Sleazy Stories

Sleazy Stories

Confessions of an infamous modern
Seducer of Women

Aaron Sleazy

Black Swallowtail Publishing

Black Swallowtail Publishing
Berlin

Revision 1.00

ISBN 978-3-942017-00-8

To Dewayne and Terry

Contents

Preface

A character like Don Juan takes what he wants. He won't wine and dine a woman for weeks. He won't seek the approval of her friends. He won't lavish her with gifts. Instead, he will rely on his knowledge of women and his magnetic personality. Once he interacts with a woman that is receptive to him, she will be enthralled because she will instinctively know that he can give her an experience virtually no other man can. Don Juan may be fiction, but seduction is not.

I have become such a man, even though it was partly by accident. Once I believed I was destined to become a great academic. Coming from a modest background, I thought I had made it when I received a scholarship for studying toward a Master's degree at the London School of Economics. My life began to change drastically in September 2007 — but not as imagined. It was stimulating to study under some of the leading figures in my field. However, in order to keep up with the competition I had to make some sacrifices. First I split up with my girlfriend, a wonderful woman. Then I dropped my hobbies one after the other. My grades were good, but I did not really enjoy life much anymore. Putting in the extra amount of work to be among the best didn't seem to be worth it. Something had to change.

I decided to apply the 80-20 rule to my studies. With much less effort I was able to still do reasonably well. Suddenly I had much more time to spare, not to mention energy. I picked up sports again, booked yoga classes and hit the gym regularly. I also got back in the habit of going to clubs regularly, which used to be one of my favourite pastimes. I felt better than ever before.

Since I tremendously enjoyed London's vibrant nightlife it occurred to me that this was the ideal opportunity to work on something I had only fantasised about before: learning to seduce women as quickly as possible. My foundations were excellent and I was a fast learner.

I had success beyond my wildest expectations. Within months I had acquired a cult following on underground seduction forums, where I chronicled my exploits. Men from all over the world sent me emails, telling me how inspiring my posts were and how much they helped them to understand women better. People were eagerly listening to my words. I became an influential voice and gained a reputation as one of the most infamous modern seducers. I became a raunchy modern Don Juan.

Sleazy Stories is a collection of my personal highlights from 2008. The beginnings were modest, but my development was rapid. It was a hell of a ride. With this book I invite you to live vicariously through me. I hope you will enjoy it.

Aaron Sleazy

Acknowledgments

This book is devoted to Dewayne and Terry, two very special men.

I have met Dewayne on an Internet forum dedicated to seduction. Not only was he the first to take an active interest in my posts, he also quickly became a mentor. He helped me to figure out a number of very important aspects about women and about life. Without him my development would have taken much longer or not happened at all. I attribute all my early breakthroughs to his help.

Terry is a good friend of mine. I met him at the London School of Economics. Besides being an amazingly cool guy and a real joy to be around, he broadened my horizon by introducing me to fashion, various clubs and literally dozens of amazing bands. Besides, it is a blast to hang out and pull women with him.

Furthermore, I want to thank my friends Terry and Karea for commenting on a draft of this book. I really appreciate their efforts.

I also want to thank everyone who has commented on my forum posts or sent me an email. No matter whether you offered advice, asked for clarification or expressed your admiration, I have learnt something from every one of you.

Gaining a following on the Internet was an interesting experience, but ironically it was when some people began to express their disapproval if not downright hatred that I realised that my experiences were truly unique. It is not easy to provoke envy in others. Therefore I love my enemies.

A particularly heartwarming experience was receiving emails from people who told me how inspirational they found my progress. It feels good to know that I was not only in it for myself but that I have made a difference to other people's lives.

Lastly, I would like to thank those who have suggested I write a book about my adventures. Without you this might not have happened.

Notes

In front of you is a chronological account of some of my interactions with women in 2008. It is my personal year in seduction in review. The chapters usually describe single nights out. However, there are infrequent connections between chapters, mostly because some women make more than one appearance.

Names of people I have met are set in SMALL CAPITALS. This convention was inspired by texts of plays. Given the often surreal nature of my adventures it is probably fitting.

Everything in this book is true and really happened. There are no exaggerations or embellishments. I even mention the names of the night clubs and places were those events took place. In order to protect the privacy of the people involved, I have used pseudonyms like BIG HAIR or FRECKLES. Names might have been nicer, but I forgot some of them and I did not want to risk accidentally using someone's real first name.

Lastly, I want to point out that I do not intend to inspire anyone to express his or her sexuality beyond the norms of the socially acceptable. Don't complain to me if you get arrested for public indecency. I won't care.

Four make outs in a gay club

Because I had grown bored of indie rock venues I wanted to explore some new places. Having taken a liking to London's scruffy East End, I picked a night with the promising name *Trailer Trash*, which was hosted at On The Rocks. Around midnight I got in and was slightly taken aback when I realised I had paid cover charge for what was nothing more than a grimy bar with a small stage. It could hold at most three hundred people. The air was almost unbreathable, and it was packed to the brim. Then it struck me that I accidentally went to a gay and lesbian night. After less than fifteen minutes I was already thinking of leaving.

A band came up. They weren't any good, but they had two virtually naked high-heeled females singing. All they wore were hot pants and a patch of ribbon that barely covered their nipples. I did not see any harm in watching some wiggling breasts before heading to another club. The gay crowd got wild and the gig turned out to be not that bad, to be honest. After the band was done playing, the DJ took over and put on some amazing electro tracks. I vowed to forget about chasing skirts for one night and just enjoy myself. But as I took another look around I noticed some pretty girls.

Nubile was dancing in a very tempting way near one of the boxes. The urge to go after her was irresistible. Some elegant moves of mine later her butt was against my groin and she really got into it. I let her continue with it for a while before I turned her around. She looked at me expectantly, so I just kissed her. My own smoothness startled me as I was not yet used to making out with girls of the highest calibre, and especially not that quickly. Nubile noticed that I was not comfortable with the situation anymore and left.

I saw a voluptuous black woman in a red dress dancing on the stage. The contrast of the colour of her skin and her dress was intriguing and an excuse to approach her. (The true reason was that merely watching Red gave me a huge boner.) After bits of rudimentary conversation I grabbed her ass. She rubbed my crotch to retaliate. I removed her hand because I did not want her to get too excited. Instead I took her outside to avoid the distractions of the club environment. After some amusing banter and more kissing I already imagined myself sharing a bed with her.

Red brought up that she was here with a gay friend. I said she should tell him that we were going to have something to eat. With surprise she retorted, “We are?” Since girls rarely, if ever, verbally agree to fuck even when they are dying to get some cock, I had to resort to this pretence. She happily agreed to grab a bite with me. We found her friend but unfortunately he was completely strung out and needed someone to take care of him. So much for fucking Red that night. Interestingly enough she tried to argue her way out of the situation, but her gay friend refused to be left alone. She really wanted to hook up with me, though, and offered me her phone number.

I was dancing by myself for a while but could not keep my eyes off Nubile. This time she was dancing on a box, thrusting her breasts out to the beat of the music. I calmly walked over to her, made eye contact and put my hand on her inner thigh. It moved closer and closer to her crotch, which she actively encouraged by playing with my hair. She teased me twice by pretending to go for the kiss, only to retreat shortly before our lips touched. It was quite possible that she saw me making out with Red, so her reaction was no surprise at all. There was no point in continuing with her.

Right next to me there were about a dozen of heavily grinding gay guys. Amidst them two girls were dancing together, visibly enjoying being in the centre of so much testosterone. I went after them, and another guy had a similar idea. Seconds later those girls had formed a ring with us two guys. I put my arm around Big Hair's waist. Her hand quickly wandered down to my lower back. I pulled her in. The other guy was also quick on his feet. As I dragged Big Hair off I saw him making out with his girl.

The music at On The Rocks was too loud to have a conversation and the outdoor area was too crowded. I decided to have some fun with Big Hair inside instead. We were heavily making out while she was humping my leg. At the same time I was playing with her heavy breasts. Furthermore, her skirt made it easy to check the level of her arousal. According to her labia it was substantial. I considered fingering her but decided to try something else. Unfortunately a friend of hers appeared out of nowhere and dragged her off before I could continue. Big Hair promised to be back in a minute.

I looked around for a new girl. PILLS was quite a cutie. She seemed to like me and asked me who I was. I told her I was Prince Charming and walked off. Because I expected BIG HAIR to be back soon it would have been unwise to work on another girl. I made a mental note to get back to her later, though.

BIG HAIR returned and was as horny as before. I immediately ushered her into a corner where she was pressing her body against mine. Kissing, grinding and feeling her up were all good fun, but there was more to be had. I guided her hand down toward my crotch. She took the hint and massaged my cock through my pants. BIG HAIR loved the feeling of it getting hard. After some moments of this it was time to shift gears again, so I put her hand back on my chest and steered it down into my pants. Her nails were gently scratching their way down to my cock, which was in eager anticipation.

Then the most unlikely thing happened. Some random asshole tapped me on the shoulder and asked for a cigarette. BIG HAIR was slightly shocked by it and immediately removed her hand from my pants. I shouted at him, "What?" He pissed me off beyond belief and I stared him down. The muscles in my right arm were tensing up. He walked off. The bubble me and this girl were in had burst. Intuitively I embraced her, but not for long because her friend showed up again to drag her off. BIG HAIR gestured that she would be right back.

Through picking up women I have learnt a lot about myself. Some of the discoveries were not always pleasant. I was annoyed that someone had messed with my chances of getting a handjob. Then this guy walked up to me and again asked for a cigarette. I could not believe this was happening so I did not say anything. His non-sequitur was to ask for a lighter. What an idiot! To be fair, he probably was just really wasted. Yet, in the heat of the moment I came to the brink of socking him. I had to get away from him immediately or else I would have lost my temper.

After I had calmed down I looked for Big Hair. She was outside in the smoking area with a gay guy who turned out to be her best friend. I commented that he and Big Hair had the same haircut, and he told me he had copied it from Nikki Sixx from Mötley Crüe. I was not yet sure how to spell any of those names, but I was pretty sure that I would not have to take him seriously. With such people it is really easy to banter, though. Both ate up my suggestion that they should form their own band. Big Hair loved the idea and went off on a tangent to talk about The White Stripes who consist of a guy and a girl. I did not have time to think much about where to take this conversation because Frantic interrupted. She wanted Big Hair and Nikki to immediately leave the club with her. I was unaware that Frantic was even part of Big Hair's group, which was partly because the club was so crowded. She was very hectic and literally ushered the two to come with her. Big Hair got up, hugged me and said I could be her biggest fan.

I found Big Hair to be fairly cool and wanted to stay in touch with her. Her phone was broken so she suggested I write down my number on her arm with a pen. But I did not have a pen with me. Frantic cut in again and shouted that they *really* had to go now. She might have been on drugs. I told her to calm down because we would only need a moment. This shut her up and pissed her off. She left, but not without a "screw you!" Nikki offered to take my number for Big Hair.

It was late already but I wanted to check up on Pills again. She had not forgotten about me either. I took her hand, spun her around and made out with her. I probably could have made out with her instantly. The odd thing about her, though, was that her kisses tasted sweet like sugar. Our of curiosity I sucked on her neck, which had the same taste. (This is a symptom of diabetes, in case you are wondering.) I did not have much time to enjoy this interaction because one of her female friends tried to push me away and told me to leave PILLS alone. I confronted her about her unacceptable behaviour and she said that she wasn't being hostile but only concerned because this was the first time her friend had taken pills. Ethics were never my strong suit, so I shrugged it off and went after PILLS regardless. But as we were about to kiss again she stopped and pressed both hands against her ears. Her upper body cringed. Apparently she was experiencing some kind of pain. This was very unfortunate — but it was time to go home anyway.

This night was my first of many in this particular scene. On the other hand, BIG HAIR was a regular. In the subsequent months I frequently bumped into her and her entourage. I also met RED again. We went on a date several days later and she was pretty much into me, buying me drinks and trying hard to please. Somehow I wasn't turned on enough, though.

A bouncer stormed into the bathroom

London's grey and cloudy skies could not keep me from going out, but Monday nights were often difficult. I knew of a student night at Eclipse. There was no queue and there were barely any people inside. As I wanted to check out the few girls in the club, a bouncer stepped up to me and tried to order me to leave my coat at the cloakroom. After a quick look around I decided that it was better to leave than to waste more money. Outside I bumped into a merry group of three, two gays and one lesbian. After some bantering they invited me to join them. They said they could get me into a club for free. The club turned out to be the Astoria, the biggest gay club in London if not Europe.

In the lobby I was offered £100 for a two-minute striptease. The money surely was tempting but I found the presence of a cameraman with full equipment suspicious. Inhibitions were not my main concern because I was doing live modelling for fine arts students. But as I stepped into the main room I saw three huge screens showing a reel of past striptease performances. This was a bit too much for me.

The girl in my group seemed to know everybody in this place, or maybe she was just very talkative. She introduced me to a number of people, but I was not overly interested in any of them. Besides, I can make friends myself. There was not much on offer except for Cocoa, a gorgeous black woman who was dancing on the stage. I joined her for a bit.

The Astoria just did not fill up. Since it is hard to have a great time in a desolate club I considered either going home or looking for another place. I could only think of two more, The End and Ghetto. The former was a fairly preposterous venue. Once they turned me down at the door because of my bland outfit. That I had intended to dance half-naked did not interest them at all. Thus I decided to try Ghetto, which turned out to be yet another predominantly gay venue. Those places have lesbians in them as well. Alas, grinding your hard cock against their asses is great fun and I love doing it.

After chatting to and dancing with a couple of girls at Ghetto but not really getting anywhere I bumped into Petite. We bantered for a bit. To my great surprise we were then interrupted by Cocoa who walked up to me and hugged me enthusiastically. Apparently those two girls were friends. After a while I left them because I wanted to check out the rest of the club. As I turned back to the dance floor I spotted Cocoa again. She was making out with an eerily androgynous creature. I really could not tell whether it was a guy or a girl. Petite slid up to me and commented that it crept her out. We both watched in a mixture of amusement and bewilderment. It slowly dawned on me that Petite was into me because she just didn't leave me. She invited me to go outside "for a smoke" but I was not thinking quickly enough and said I didn't smoke. It had not yet occurred to me that you could do all kinds of kinky stuff in dark alleys.

Cocoa rejoined us. She was dancing seductively in front of me.

The process was simple and straightforward: kissing, dancing, grinding. We made out heavily and she was a very good kisser. I put her hand on my crotch and moments later I slipped my hand inside her underpants to work her buttocks with the intention of indirectly stimulating her labia. Then I put a finger in her ass crack. We had barely spoken to each other but maybe you don't really need to talk to women to get them? I put her hands on my belly and her fingers quickly wandered into my pants. She only played with my pubic hair to tease me, though.

To leave COCOA wanting more I danced with some other girls in a completely nonchalant fashion. When I was looking for her again she was taking pictures with her friend PETITE. They both took turns striking provocative poses. I did not feel like waiting any longer and I tongued COCOA down while she was pouting at the camera. We were all over each other in an instant. After maybe one or two minutes she announced that she had to go to the toilet. Because one of her hands was resting on my left thigh, dangerously close to my dick, I offered to join her.

Inside the ladies' toilet I pushed her against the wall. We made out passionately. Playfully she asked me whether I was supposed to be in here. I ignored this comment and reinitiated kissing. She giggled, visibly enjoying the moment. Two other girls came in and stared at us in disbelief. COCOA's hand came closer and closer to my dick. Now I only had to get her into one of the stalls. I took her hand and wanted to lead her off. Suddenly I felt a strong hand resting on my shoulder. As I turned around and saw a huge black bouncer. He nonchalantly told me that the men's toilet was somewhere else. I can't say that I particularly liked his kind of humour. With a quick movement of his head he gestured me to walk outside. I felt destroyed. After wallflowering in a depressed mood for a couple of minutes

I decided to leave.

Next to the staircase to the exit Cocoa was excitedly talking to her friend. As she saw me walking by she threw an arm around me and asked me where I was going. She had a huge smile on her face. When I said I was on my way home she gave me a disappointed look. We hugged and kissed, and on my way home I mentally slapped myself for not pushing the interaction further. The aftertaste of the confrontation with the bouncer had clouded my judgement. I could have tried to take Cocoa home, or at the very least gotten her number. It was a great night nonetheless and it hinted at what was in store for me in terms of seduction.

She was already sitting on my bed

Among the benefits of living in university accommodation was that you could walk into the kitchen on your floor and bump into an Asian girl that was not there the day before. She was from Taiwan and I shall call her HAZEL. She was hotter than pretty much every girl I had met at my nerdy university so far.

HAZEL was preparing a bowl of soup. Asking her whether she was a tourist prompted her to tell me her story. She was in London for a short spring course at Saint Martin's College. We bantered for a while and got along great. After about fifteen minutes I decided to pull out some sexual material, which made her talk about her last relationship.

One of the guys on my floor walked into the kitchen. He did not say a word, but the next day he asked me whether HAZEL was a friend of mine. Apparently our conversation did not seem like one of strangers. Indeed, this girl was completely hooked throughout the interaction. I only had to play it cool by leaning against the wall while she was stirring her soup. The problem at hand, though, was how to get her to have sex with me. By keeping her talking *about* sex I was at least moving the interaction in the right direction. She suggested to sit down.

Hazel said she liked to dominate men in relationships and that her ex-boyfriend was a "pussy." I actually made her use this word. She kept using it after I had introduced it with, "In all honesty, to me he doesn't sound like much of a man but more like a pussy." The topic changed to dominance in the bedroom. I got the impression that her claiming to want to dominate men was nonsense and wanted to test my hypothesis. When she was fiddling with the cutlery I took the fork out of her hand with the words, "Would you please stop it!" She abruptly did, averted her gaze and giggled. Unfortunately I had to leave soon afterwards.

I had promised to go out with some acquaintances from Belgium. Blowing them off would have been the better course of action, but I prefer keeping my word. However, I wanted to continue with Hazel and took her number. We agreed to hang out some other time. By the way, we sat there for well over an hour and not once did she touch her food.

The next day, after a fairly uneventful night out, I thought of Hazel. I walked down the hallway and knocked on her door. She was still in her pyjamas and sleepy. With bigger balls I would have invited myself in, but they had yet to grow to an appropriate size. She said she would knock on my door later. After four to five hours she indeed did.

Girls can't just knock on your door when they want to fuck. There has to be a pretence. Hers was that she had "just made some tea and thought I'd drop by." It was a ridiculous excuse because the kitchen was halfway *between* our rooms on the corridor. As I opened the door she seemed slightly nervous. I was getting a hard-on while I let her in.

There was only one chair in my room, so she had to sit down on my bed. We briefly talked about plans for tonight and I invited her to go to a club with me. She replied that in general she rather enjoyed spending her time alone. I was going out up to five times a week and this girl told me she goes out two to four times *per year*! It did not bother me because I was working towards fucking her in my room anyway. With some less than subtle steering the conversation drifted towards sex.

I dropped that the walls in this building were rather thin and that you could therefore hear practically everything your neighbours were doing. Of course I did not mention that the London School of Economics was full of nerds who probably would not know what to do with a woman if one accidentally knocked at their door and literally begged for it. "But how do you guys have sex in here if you hear everything your neighbours are doing?", she asked. "People on this floor don't exactly have a lot of sex," I replied.

She talked about her time living in dorms in Japan or Hong Kong and how people there arrange to have sex. This was interesting because it showed what was on her mind. "Usually two people share a room, and if you want to have sex you have to do it when your roommate is away," she revealed. She explained that in this case you just put both beds together. After the act your roommate might not be too pleased when discovering suspicious stains on the sheets, though.

"But gays and lesbians have a clear advantage. They just have to say that they want to share a room and if this works out they are free to do whatever they want to do. You know, it's like this: if you and me wanted to share a room, we would just have to say so, and we could." This was clear nonsense because, as she had said before, the floors in those dorms were strictly single sex.

We had spent about twenty minutes talking to each other. There had not been much touching yet, but I felt that I was on the right track because we were vividly talking about sex. I told her about my idea of the magic of the moment and that one should always act on impulses. She excitedly agreed. In my mind I was already ravaging her.

However, by telling her about Cocoa and the bouncer that interrupted us in the toilet I completely wrecked the situation. For some reason I thought it would be a fitting story to tell, but apparently it wasn't. After I had finished, Hazel made a frantic excuse and hurriedly left: "I better go back to my room. … You've got my email address. Just add me on Facebook and we will keep in touch." Damn.

This taught me that picking up girls is a bit like playing chess. If you make a blunder it does not matter that you have had a winning position.

"Do you want to fuck me?"

Due to a lack of options on Mondays I went to The End. The night started slowly and it took me quite a while to get used to the atmosphere. Then I ran into a couple of guys I vaguely knew. One of them, DR. YEN, walked up to me to tell me I was a monster. My reputation apparently exceeded my actual level of skill. At around 1.30 a.m. most of those guys had formed a circle, presumably discussing pick-up instead of approaching girls.

I saw SUNSHINE walking by. She looked luscious, so I grabbed her hand and said, "I don't think we have met before." We spent some happy moments chatting, caressing and hugging each other. Because I had stopped her on the way to the ladies' room, she had to leave me for a moment but promised to be back. In the meantime I talked to the other guys. SUNSHINE joined our circle and asked me whether those were friends of mine. I was rather disinclined to introduce her to five guys who were out to pick up women. Therefore I dragged her off to another area of the club before she could finish her sentence. We sat down on the stage.

Earlier that day I had thought about a few amusing stories from my life to tell girls to avoid stalling in conversations. At an appropriate moment I mentioned how much I loved playing with my grandmother's cats when I was a kid. It did the trick, and SUNSHINE was listening with great interest.

"I have to tell you that I am here with a friend," she warned me all of a sudden.

"Oh, I did not know this."

"You have nothing to worry about. Just keep it in mind."

She walked off to find her friend. One of my acquaintances saw an opportunity and tried his luck. I consider such behaviour bad etiquette. It did not matter because he fell flat on his face. He apologised later on.

Since SUNSHINE was gone for a while I had to entertain myself. I was dancing and poking the tummies of random girls for giggles. Among them was KISSES. She had already walked away from her friends and was leaning against a pillar. Her face was very pretty but to say the same about her body would have been a bit of a stretch. Because I was bored I walked up to her. This was enough to put her into a trance. Our lips were close, but I was only teasing her. She was enthralled and deeply gazed into my eyes. "Just kiss me," she begged me.

She literally stood there with her mouth gaping wide open. Because I had nothing better to do we made out for a while. I did not want to push things too far, though, because of SUNSHINE. After all, it is within reason to chase after a prettier bird in the bush when you've got only a plump one in your hand. KISSES was keen on getting me but I preferred to walk off. She kept staring at me and demonstratively blew off a couple of guys in plain sight of me. Hopefully she met someone else that night. I had more important things to take care off, like scoring with a particularly sexy Swedish girl named SUNSHINE.

After dancing for a while to get my mind off KISSES, I looked around for SUNSHINE. She was talking to the friend she previously mentioned. I pulled her in and danced with her. I spun her around. Then I dipped and dry-humped her until she broke a sweat. I was dominant as fuck. She got completely into it and added a cool variation on her own: she put her legs around my waist and quickly bent over backwards so that I had to carry all her weight. Luckily I am in a pretty decent shape. She loved it. But she had other needs as well. "I need some drugs. Do you have some coke?", she suddenly asked. (I don't do drugs, even though many believe the opposite to be the case.) Because I had none, she wandered off, looking for a supplier.

Two random guys sensed an easy prey and cornered her. One tried the infamous back attack and pressed his groin against this unsuspecting female's butt. She pushed him away immediately. I joined her and we picked things up right where we had left off. "I like this a lot!", she said, and after a short pause she asked me where I lived. Earlier that week a girl had asked me the same question with the obvious intention of going to my place to get her brains fucked out. I have learnt my lesson and instead of giving SUNSHINE a lengthy description I told her I was living "just around the corner." "That was easy," she replied. Everything was fine. But two seconds later I almost lost my composure. "Do you want to fuck me?", she asked me.

With arguably too much excitement I said, "Yes!" Such enthusiasm can kill your chances, so I steered back. Some girls are content with simply knowing that they could get the guy. Once he lets out that he wants to have sex with her, it is game over for him. I quickly added, “Maybe I want to.” She smiled gleefully.

We kept dancing. SUNSHINE turned around and ground her ass against my dick. A little bit later she rubbed and squeezed it. When I guided her other hand up to my head she pulled my hair like crazy, which got me to the brink of screaming. In order to keep the tension I gently pushed her away.

“I want some coke!”, she protested.

“You’ll do fine without drugs tonight, baby.”

This was a cheesy line but she did not bring up the topic again. Later on she even said that she wouldn’t need anything tonight. However, I have reason to suspect that she snorted a line somewhere in between.

Eventually she wanted to go back to her place. But when I told her that we could just leave she brought up her friend again. She walked off to fill him in. Since she kept me waiting for longer than I expected I went looking for her. I found her in a deep discussion with her friend. When I showed up the guy immediately walked off. I sat down next to her. Her friend, a gay guy, was annoyed because she wanted to hook up. It did not seem bother her at all. “I am ready to leave. You can come with me if you want,” she said.

So far this might seem like an excessively easy pick-up. At the bus stop, however, the ride became bumpy. “So, why exactly do you want to come home with me? You don’t even know me,” she said. Obviously I would have shot myself in the foot had I told her it was because of her looks, so I said I liked her energy and how we danced together. Those were valid reasons, nonetheless.

On the bus she threw me another nasty curveball and asked me whether I loved someone. "I love no one. … I love life," I answered. Looking sceptically at me she hissed that I should not give her "any of this bullshit." I replied that it was true. SUNSHINE then fessed up that she was still in love with someone she had broken up years ago. (Probably she got dumped.) This hinted at some troubles ahead. I did not dwell on the topic and she dropped it soon. Letting her talk about how much she was still in love with her ex-boyfriend would hardly have helped me.

After we got off the bus she wanted to buy some chocolate at a nearby gas station. This was when I realised that I only had one condom with me. I wanted to stack up and get a couple of extra large ones but they did not have any. Instead I bought some regular ones, but those usually lead to a rather bad experience. SUNSHINE got curious.

"What did you buy? I thought you said you had some condoms. Were you lying?"

"I only have one left so I bought some more. But they did not have large ones."

"Oh, wait.... How big are you then?"

"Bigger than average."

She kept needling me about the size of my cock for quite some time but I did not tell her. She would soon see it in all its glory anyway.

At her house she made me some tea, showed me random pictures of herself and even brought me a plate full of delicious food. This girl treated me like a king. Something was wrong here, I thought. Because why be so nice to someone you only want to have a one-night stand with?

I liked this girl. I used to think that women who treat you nicely only do so because they don't want to feel like sluts. However, I have later learnt that they have no scruples about using you only for your penis if this is all they desire. I was too concerned about "being in control" and thus acted aloof. This meant that I blew a chance to get to know someone as a person.

We ended up playing around in her bed. Our clothes went off progressively. Eventually we were in our underwear. I paused to take a look at her body and completely undressed her. She was really beautiful. The mood was still playful, so she blurted out, "Come on, I wanna see your big cock!" I told her to get it out of my pants, which she instantly pulled down. SUNSHINE took it into her hands and eagerly watched it getting bigger. I still played it cool. Instead I should have pinned her down and railed her right there. We took a break to eat some more. Because I felt stuffed I lied down and we cuddled for a bit.

Suddenly SUNSHINE said she did not want to fuck anymore. This was probably because she started to like me, which made her worry I would think she was a slut if she "gave it up" too quickly. Fucking girls ASAP takes care of that problem but I had missed that boat. It got even more bizarre when she announced that she did not want to kiss me anymore. This was really odd. I had no explanation, but her reasons became clear in an instant. She had a minor nervous breakdown and started to cry. Shit.

While crying she told me much more than I would have wanted to know about her problems of finding a decent guy. I did not dwell on any of the topics she brought up but only said that everything would be all right. After what felt like an eternity she calmed down and said she only wanted to chill. I had not gotten any action so far and I honestly did not care anymore. I even contemplated going home, but public transport in London in the early morning hours was such a mess that I decided to stick it out.

"How come you feel so comfortable lying next to a naked girl?", she suddenly asked me, insinuating that I was picking up girls left, right and centre. "Come on, it's not such a big deal," I replied. We were lying right next to each other without saying a word and caressing each other's faces.

"I just want to get some sleep," she said. "That's fine with me. I could use some rest as well." I wish I had counted the seconds. Almost immediately after I had rolled away, her body was rubbing up against mine. "Do you want to fuck?", she cooed. In a completely calm tone of voice I said, "Sure, why not?" I got on top of her and tried to kiss her. "Don't kiss me. You can fuck me if you want but don't kiss me."

She was hugely turned on, scratched my back and pulled my hair like crazy. I put my middle finger in and realised she was dripping wet. She could not have gotten that horny in such a short amount of time. Then it struck me that she probably found my utter lack of care so arousing. SUNSHINE grabbed my cock and whacked it while I was shoving my tongue down her throat. I stopped and told her to suck it. She refused. In her hands my cock got bigger and bigger. "Just fuck me!", she begged.

SUNSHINE kept staring at my cock and said she would start to scream when I put it in her. I really do love fellatio, though, so I put my cock close to her lips. Reflexively she kissed it all over. I let her do that for a while but eventually I shoved it into her mouth. She sucked it enthusiastically. After a while I took over, grabbed her hair and fucked her head with a few good thrusts. She got immensely turned on by this, moaned louder and louder and arched her back. I reached for her pussy with my other hand.

I kept a firm grip on her blonde mane and yanked her head back and forth while I was administering forceful thrusts with my pelvis. In irregular intervals I shoved my cock completely down her throat. With my other hand I was playing with her clit. This certainly was not a bad position to be in. I wanted to amp her up even more, so I leaned back a bit and slowly slid two fingers in. Instead of letting out a loud moan she completely freaked out and tried to push me off.

"Honey, you are so beautiful, but I can't!", she mumbled. She rolled over and cried. I told her no matter what the problem was, it was all right because I would not judge her in any way. "You don't have to do anything you don't want to do," I added. Again she brought up her ex-boyfriend. She also revealed the number of guys she had slept with. Her count was fifty. It did not bother me at all. After fifteen minutes or so she finally calmed down. It was about 6 a.m. and I was getting really tired. We were once again lying right next to each other.

Suddenly there was a calmness in the air and everything seemed to be perfectly fine. She rolled over to me and put her head on my chest. Her hand wandered down to my groin and she said I had "the most beautiful cock" while touching it with her fingertips. I put her hand on it and she happily jerked me off. I blew a decent load after a few minutes and she cleaned up the mess. After all that drama I did not really give a damn about fucking her properly so I left things at that.

Sunshine cuddled up to me again. She put my hand on her pussy, indicating that I should rub her clit. It did not take her long to get into it. Moments later I felt a certain urge. Because she freaked out earlier, I whispered in her ear that I would love to finger her. She moaned lightly and told me to just do it. Her reward was a thorough A-spot massage, while I was working her clit with the middle finger of my other hand. After a few minutes her pussy began to clamp down on my fingers rhythmically. She was moaning loudly while twisting her body. When it got too much for her she pulled my hair and scratched my back. It was almost violent and I got a huge kick out of it. She was moaning louder and louder. Yet, it seemed as if she had problems climaxing. Despite all my efforts she just did not come. Eventually she said she could not completely relax but that it felt awesome nonetheless. I kept going — and a little bit later she experienced what looked like a decent orgasm. It came in multiple waves. She may even have squirted a little bit. I am quite sure that a small load splashed against the palm of my hand but I could not verify it because she had only lit some candles.

Afterwards she cuddled up to me again. We were lying there in post-coital bliss for a while. Then she asked me whether I like "going to clubs and picking up fit girls." I said maybe. She laughed. After a pause she playfully slapped my chest and asked, "How can there be a maybe?"

Because I'm so different

Terry had given me a complete fashion makeover the week before, which took great inspiration from bands such as The Horrors. In his words, the declared goal was to "shamelessly rip off the most fashionable people in London and somehow come up with something unique." He succeeded and I was now walking around in skinny jeans and a generally flamboyant outfit. This was not much of a problem at the flat party I had been to earlier that night, because I was mostly sitting around. But when I went to Bar Music Hall later on, I realised I could not yet dance in this outfit.

Since it was past 1 a.m. already I could not afford to waste any time. I was not sure whether the girl I was talking to was genuinely interested or only looking for validation. To get some clarity on this question I squeezed her ass. She acted slightly embarrassed. After I smirkingly told her that there was no reason to be shy, she hastily returned to her friends. The next few interactions were similarly successful.

I was running out of time and women to approach, but there were two more girls on the dance floor. One of them, Tomboy, seemed somewhat inhibited, but she certainly had nice boobs. I took her hand and pulled her in. Within seconds I could feel the sexual tension between us. I quickly capitalised on it. Luckily there were some comfortable leather chairs nearby. I sat down and pulled her into my lap. She seemed to find me very attractive and asked the usual questions: "What's your name?", "Where are you from?", and, "What do you do for a living?"

I told her about some of my experiences in Berlin, which always got a good reaction. It was also a great opportunity to steer the conversation toward sex. When she asked me about the Love Parade I threw in that there wouldn't be one this year because it had been such a mess in recent years with all those people fucking in the streets. This made her giggle.

After some mutual caressing we continued with light kissing. I did not want her to think it was a done deal so I teased her a bit to keep her on her toes. "Psycho Killer" by The Talking Heads came on and she excitedly said that she loved the eighties. I told her I liked that song as well, but also that it was actually from the seventies. This was a good excuse for playfully slapping her ass. She liked it.

Tomboy got up and gestured me to follow her. She wanted to introduce me to her friend. We exchanged some niceties but I could not really be bothered and sat down again. They had "the conversation" and were discussing whether I was worthy of getting Tomboy. Apparently I was, because her friend left soon afterwards. Amidst some rather pointless conversation it emerged that her flat was within walking distance.

At Bar Music Hall the lights go on about ten minutes before the music stops. This was now, and Tomboy seemed somewhat shocked when she saw me in bright light.

"Oh my God, you're really young. … How old are you?", she blurted out.

"What do you think?"

"Um…. Maybe twenty-five?"

I moved my lips very close to her ear and whispered, "Tonight, I'll be as old as you want me to be."

I could not believe I had said those words. Anyway, I told Tomboy to get her stuff. She got up and put on her jacket. Then Madonna's "Like a Prayer" came on and she suggested a dance. Halfway through the song I told her once again that it was time to get out of here. Because she did not react at all I took her hand and led her to the exit. Outside Bar Music Hall I pushed her against the wall and made out with her. Afterwards we held eye contact but I deliberately did not kiss her.

As we came close to a bus station she stopped and took both of my hands. I have been in such situations before. They were painful. Before I had figured out how to get women I nonetheless had a couple of dates that went fairly well. I could sense that the girl wanted me, but because I had no idea how to make things happen I have heard sentences like, "Thanks for a lovely evening!", far too often, only to never see any of those girls again. It seemed that Tomboy was about to pull a similar move, but I preempted it by lifting her up. In this position we made out for a bit before I put her down again and led her *somewhere*. I did not know where her flat was and thus had no idea where I was going. Luckily, she guided me when necessary. I almost had to laugh.

At her place she put up some resistance. She seemed to like me and was all over me. Yet, she was reluctant to take things to the bedroom. We probably spent an hour on the sofa in her living room. Eventually she embraced me and looked me deep in my eyes.

“Who were you with tonight?”, she asked in a sincere voice.

“I was out on my own.”

“Do you often go out on your own?”

The implication was obvious.

“I was at a flat party before. It was all right but not great, so I wanted to go somewhere else afterwards.”

“Is that so?”

“Yeah. I mean, just think of it: because of this you got lucky to meet me tonight.”

“I got lucky?”, she said and laughed.

We made out some more. Finally she seemed ready. I asked her where the bedroom was. She pointed into the direction. I took her there, threw her on the bed and told her to get me out of my clothes.

Taking a walk with a new friend

In the morning a lively Korean girl I had met some weeks ago contacted me via Facebook. She was in London again for a few days and suggested to meet up. I told her I would take her to one of my favourite venues. Later she texted me that she would bring a friend with her. Her friend surprisingly turned out to be a guy. He was a complete douche.

I wanted to take Lively to Ghetto. But because it was almost empty, we took a bus to the East End. Every bar or club there was either closed or dead, which taught me not to stray too far from Soho on a Wednesday night. While looking for a place there was some light hand holding between me and her. I could not do a lot because of her friend, even though he was almost a complete non-issue. Lively teased him by calling him "such a nice guy" and made openly fun of him by saying, "Aww, he's so sad now. There was this couple on the bus and this was too much for him because he doesn't have a girlfriend right now. … We should find one for him tonight." "Sure, why not?", I replied indifferently.

After forty-five minutes of checking out dead bars and clubs we went back to Ghetto, where the atmosphere had changed considerably. It was reasonably crowded and some hot girls were among the patrons as well. LIVELY took off her jacket and looked around helplessly. I told her the cloakroom was around the corner and off she was with her friend. I exploited this opportunity by positioning myself in the middle of the dance floor. MATRYOSHKA looked at me, so I walked over to her. As I was about to get close, the guy next to her turned his head and started talking to her. I found this confusing and thus went to the bar first to get some tap water. I don't give up that quickly, though. A few minutes later I went back and told her I knew her from somewhere.

"No, this can't be," she protested.

"But I do know you!"

"No, you don't. … I'm not a local."

"Then I have probably met your *type* before."

It turned out she was a tourist who came to London regularly. She was touching me a lot. When LIVELY returned, my fingertips had been on MATRYOSHKA's ass and breasts already. To keep up with the competition LIVELY paid an awful lot of attention to me. It was amusing to watch LIVELY trying to bond with MATRYOSHKA. MATRYOSHKA almost completely ignored her but she kept going for quite a while nonetheless. I decided to let those two girls get to know each other better and kept dancing with both. I was only waiting for a chance to leverage the circumstances.

I spotted BUMBLEBEE and LUSCIOUS, made eye contact with LUSCIOUS and held my hand up. After a high-five I pulled her in. BUMBLEBEE walked off, which was almost too easy. LUSCIOUS quickly got really into me. She turned around to rub her ass against my crotch. In the middle of a short token conversation I softly kissed her on the lips and led her off the dance floor to sit down. At first she seemed reluctant, and her English was almost incomprehensible. On the plus side, though, her legs looked good resting on mine. After a few more minutes she announced that she had to go back to her friends, which was fine with me.

We rejoined her group. Luscious introduced me to Bumblebee and then we danced some more. She really loved to arouse me. It was awfully hot in the club so I told her we should catch some fresh air, but she was not up for it. I wanted to drag her outside regardless, but someone else intervened. It was Skinny. She was a real stunner and ticked all my boxes. Her face was beautiful and her proportions just perfect. Despite her skinny frame she had spectacularly full and well-shaped breasts.

Skinny was the sister of Luscious, and she didn't like the creep (me) who was hitting on her at all. "That's my sister, let her go!", she demanded, while slapping my chest and upper arms with her palms. Her English was atrociously bad and what she really said was more like, "Sister mine, let go!" I had to laugh.

My original intention was to get rid of Skinny because I wanted to continue with her sister. But then I saw that her eyes began to sparkle and her pupils were dilating. I immediately let go of any thoughts about Luscious and focused my attention on her even more attractive sister. We kissed almost immediately. "It's really hot in here. Let's go outside," I told her. Rather than waiting for an answer I simply dragged her out of the club. She willingly came with me. This time nobody interfered.

Outside I gave her a hug before leading her around the corner. More kissing, hugging and chatting ensued. "I really like you," she said. This was my cue to put her hand on my crotch. She rubbed it and moaned quietly. Skinny was ready to go. I led her hands over my belt. She hastily unbuckled it and moments later her tiny hands were inside my pants, playing with my cock. Less than ten minutes of meeting her she was giving me a handjob. It was almost too good to be true.

She suddenly wanted to get back inside. Maybe it was a bit too much for her. I decided to get her number, because you never know. On the short walk back to Ghetto I thought, "This can't be it! She was moaning and literally begging for it moments ago." Given those circumstances I was unwilling to settle for just a number. I gave her another hug and we kissed again. "I live ten minutes from here. Why don't we go for a walk?", I asked rhetorically. She came with me.

Skinny was one of the hottest girls I ever had interacted with and within fifteen minutes we were walking back to my place. It was fairly exciting. Things went smoothly only for a while, though. After a few minutes she abruptly stopped. "I have to go back to my friends!", she protested. "That's fine. My place is very close, we'll be right back."

Her high heels ensured that the way back to my place took us much longer than expected. I told her some of my prepared stories, episodes from my life: childhood, cats, parks, how I enjoy lying in green grass and letting the wind blow all over my face and all that stuff. We talked, laughed, cuddled, kissed. I also made sure to give her a pretence for going back to my place, which was to "watch a short video."

Skinny was extremely attracted to me, yet she seemingly did not want to have sex that quickly. Unfortunately she got second thoughts. A mere five hundred metres from my place she said,

"I can't do this. I have to go back and find my friends." I hugged and kissed her while telling her that it would be fine. This got her a few metres further. About twenty metres from my place she stopped again. Time for more hugs and kisses. She asked me where we were. I partly ignored her question and told her, "It's right over there." But the closer we came to my flat, the more resistance she put up. Eventually she turned around and walked back to the club.

This could not have been it. I lifted her up. "OK!", she said. We kissed again. "God, this feels so good, doesn't it?", I whispered in her ear. Five minutes later we were in front of the building. I inserted my key card and was about to open the door.

"I can't do this. I don't want to have sex."

"Where does that come from? Nobody said we were going to have sex."

"This is too soon. We can meet up tomorrow, but today is no good."

We walked back to the club. As we were about twenty metres away from my place I hugged her again. She tried to kiss me passionately, but I deflected her attempt and shoved her hand down my pants instead. "God, this feels so good. … I want you so much. … Imagine how good we would feel together," I said. SKINNY was moaning. She did not want to change the direction, though. It took us ages to get back to Ghetto because she kept rubbing my cock inside my pants.

We passed a dark alley. SKINNY was still in massive heat, so I led her there after she had tongued me down yet again. We sat down, kissed and cuddled. This went on for a while. Eventually I thought it was appropriate to pull my cock out. She happily whacked it, and she really knew how. Maybe it were her tiny hands and small fingers that made it feel so good. After a few minutes she stopped. "Sorry, I can't do it," she said. Of course she could. I put her hand back on it and she continued working it. However, the moment my cock began to throb she quickly retracted her hand and said, "I'm sorry, I have to go back to the club and find my friends."

Since I did not see a point in persisting I led her back to the club. We chatted some more and agreed to meet in front of a nearby Starbucks the following day. Because her English was fairly bad I led her to that particular coffee shop so that she knew where it was. We sealed this with a "pinky swear." Back in the club we danced some more. She rubbed my cock some more and we kissed some more. Eventually her friends showed up and took her with them.

After SKINNY was gone I took the number of MATRYOSHKA, and I saw that LIVELY had hooked up with somebody. I was pretty sure she did it out of jealousy. If I interpreted the situation correctly she went home with this guy, leaving her overly nice friend alone. It was unfortunate that things worked out this way. I might have had a chance with her that night, had I focused on her. But I preferred trying my luck with SKINNY because I found her more attractive. Nothing ventured, nothing gained.

Fun at a fetish party

Always looking for new experiences I decided to go to a huge fetish party called *Torture Garden*, and I had no idea what to expect. In the queue I chatted up DOMINATRIX, a woman in her mid-thirties. When two female friends of hers joined us, she immediately introduced me to them and told them how cool I was. Then she opened her purse to get her lipstick. It was certainly arousing when she put it on suggestively right in front of me, but an even greater turn-on was that her purse was stuffed with condoms. She literally shoved them in my face.

Inside the venue I felt uncomfortable at first. According to the policy you were not allowed to touch anyone without their explicit prior consent. It also said that you had to "show respect for everyone" or something like that. Unable to figure out how to hit on girls under those conditions, I wandered around aimlessly for about an hour. I was at a complete loss. Cover charge was over £30 and I was not going to risk this investment lightly. Luckily I bumped into my friend DR. YEN.

"Dude, I have no idea what I can or can't do in this place. I mean, how am I supposed to get anywhere when I'm not allowed to touch them?", I asked him in despair.

"Don't worry. This is just to distract gropers and the like. It's all right to touch the girls."

After this exchange things went much better. I had to get into a good mood first, so I danced by myself for a while. A girl was dancing on her own in a corner, and only in underwear no less. She was extraordinarily beautiful. Well, her body was, but according to her face she was in her mid-thirties. (There were hardly any young people around.) The conversation with her went fine until she demanded I stop touching her. I don't think she was too serious about it, though. When talking about tattoos she asked me whether I had any. I pointed at my crotch and said I had one on my dick that changes as it gets harder and offered to show it to her.

She stared expectantly at my crotch and expected me to pull my cock out. I said I couldn't show it to her because I didn't know her well enough yet. Probably it would have been a good idea to just whip it out. After all, we were in a dark corner already. Afterwards the conversation stalled. In case you are wondering: no, I don't have a tattoo on my cock.

I bumped into DOMINATRIX' group again. She excitedly walked up to me and kissed me on the cheek. Unfortunately I still felt too intimidated by the environment to capitalise on this opportunity. Nonetheless, we had a lot of fun on the dance floor. PĄCZKI joined us for one song. She looked over at me a couple of times afterwards. She, too, had melon-sized breasts that were about the size of her head and was only wearing lingerie. I decided to go after her.

PĄCZKI was quite receptive to my touch and pressed her body against mine while talking to me. I instinctively put my hand on her naked ass. When I tried to kiss her she told me her boyfriend was in the venue. He was standing right behind us, actually. He was built like a stallion and about two metres tall. I did not flinch at all. She continued with, "…but he doesn't mind!", only to heavily make out with me afterwards. CONAN didn't care about it at all. After a few minutes she asked me where my girlfriends were, and when I told her they were probably dancing somewhere, she responded, "They were so beautiful. Come, bring them here!"

I walked off, looking for DOMINATRIX and her friends. Looking back, I think I should have dragged PĄCZKI off with a line like, "Sure, let's look for them," while pulling her into a dark corner. I bumped into her a couple of times later, and every time she was fairly aggressive. She slapped or rubbed my ass or pinched my nipples, but I had yet to learn how to deal with the pressure of such situations.

Then I met LOLLIPOP. She was even more amazing than the last girl, despite not having fake breasts. Her face was very pretty and she had an astoundingly tight body. When she saw me she made warm eye contact and licked her lollipop in a rather suggestive way. She offered it to me. I playfully hesitated for a while before I licked it. Afterwards I put it on her lips. She licked it again, but as if she was licking the tip of a cock. Some girls are just great! I put her hand away, pulled her in and made out with her. After some random conversation I decided to turn things sexual.

"You know, I think you are kind of cute," I said and grabbed her firm ass. This made me realise that she was not wearing any underwear under her skimpy PVC skirt. In response she pressed her nubile body against mine. Being investigative, I checked how horny she was by moving my middle finger toward her pussy. She was wet. I massaged her labia, which she did not particularly mind. My fingers then explored her vagina for a while.

Someone was walking toward us. "Here comes my boyfriend. What's your name?", LOLLIPOP frantically whispered in my ear. I told her and she subsequently introduced me to him. After turning to me again and asking where I was from she gave him another piece of information and added, "...and he is from Germany."

I shook his hand, but I don't know whether he noticed the warm liquid on my fingers. This guy was tall and scrawny and definitely no match for me, so I cared even less. The moment he let go of my hand I put it on LOLLIPOP's ass again and continued with rubbing her pussy from behind. This was all good fun, but with her boyfriend nearby she felt uncomfortable. After one or two minutes she said she had to leave. She excitedly accepted my offer to dance with her later on, though. When I told this part of the story to TERRY the next day he dryly commented, "Good job on the pussy rubbing but it does seem kind of whack that you had to pay £30 for it." He had a good point.

I felt like taking another look around the party. Despite the wild claims on their website and on certain Internet forums, the atmosphere was quite stiff. Rather than the wild debauchery I had expected, people seemed somewhat reserved. A few were having sex in the open, but those were mostly couples, if matching outfits and the absence of condoms were reliable indicators. I also ran into DOMINATRIX again, who was dragging some guy to the exit.

In the main corridor LOLLIPOP was walking past with her boyfriend. I hip-bumped her, which she answered with a smile.

Then she walked away from her guy. He had no idea what was going on and had frozen up already. I followed LOLLIPOP but was unable to come up with anything good to say to her after her playful, "What?", which she delivered to me with a huge smile. I probably should just have tongued her down. However, my balls had yet to grow.

On the dance floor I saw a drunk girl making out with a body builder in a police uniform. Her friends dragged her off. Then she saw me and wanted to kiss me on the cheek. Well, she also had huge fake breasts, but she was not that skinny. I wanted to play with her nonetheless and kissed her on the lips. Her friends panicked and dragged her off. The friends remained on the dance floor. A couple of times their friend tried to get back to me, but they always held her back or shielded her from me.

Then I bumped into BAKLAVA. She wore only high-heels, a G-string, and a corset that completely exposed her breasts. They were fake, huge and magnificent. She was one of the most attractive girls in the venue. Her long blonde wig furthermore gave her the allure of a pornstar. I completely wrecked all my chances with her, though, as I just could not stop either palming her ass, squeezing it or pressing it against my cock, or staring at her bosom in utter disbelief.

With a modicum of self-control I could have achieved much more. BAKLAVA kept touching me. Heck, I even managed to get her away from her friends. She also asked me the usual questions girls always ask. But I was unable to give proper answers. My replies were monosyllabic. I was too busy staring at her tits and grabbing her ass. Frankly, I never felt like a bigger moron while also tremendously enjoying myself at the same time. I should have dragged her off the dance floor, sat her down somewhere and worked my magic, instead of drooling over her like an idiot. Self-control was a huge issue for me that evening. However, this was to be expected as I was surrounded by so many hot and practically naked women.

At 6.30 a.m. the club was already quite empty. There was only one somewhat attractive woman left. Her face was quite old, but her body looked young and fake. I could have had her. "You are so gorgeous," she said while rubbing my chest. I told her I knew that already and turned her around so that she could grind against my cock. I got hard. She giggled and turned her head. "Apparently I am starting to move you," she said. I tried to shove my tongue down her throat, but she was not having any of it and walked off. With some more patience this interaction could have gone somewhere. I shrugged because I was getting tired anyway.

A bizarre second date

Considering how open SKINNY was when I first met her, she was surprisingly reluctant on our first date. I didn't really get anywhere with her. Nonetheless I gave her another shot — because she really turned me on. We went for a walk through Westminster. She had not been to Trafalgar Square before, so I took her there and she loved it. Her primary concern was to figure out whether I was a good candidate for a relationship. It was cute that she insisted I ask someone to take a picture of us. After we had sat down on the stairs she repeatedly offered me her sandwich. I declined but she did not take no for an answer and wanted me to have some of it. While talking about things *we* could do in the future she was very touchy-feely.

The next topic she brought up was more intimate. She wanted to know about my former girlfriends. I completely ignored this part. Then she pulled out a real shocker, but keep in mind that her English was quite bad. She usually directly asked questions without transitioning. It often sounded unintentionally rude.

"Do you have diseases?", she asked me out of the blue.

"I beg your pardon. What do you mean?"

She paused, then she asked me, "Do you have AIDS?"

I looked at her incredulously, which made her pull out an electronic Korean-English dictionary. Seconds later I read "AIDS" on its display. I cracked up and she laughed as well. I playfully pinched her and told her she couldn't ask someone she barely knew such a question. "But I have to know!", she protested and said that according to her Korean friends back home AIDS was "really widespread in the West." After reassuring each other that we were clean of any STDs whatsoever we made our way to St James' Park.

We sat down on a bench. As she had done on the previous date she insisted that she could only hug and kiss boyfriends and not friends. This arguably meant that if she "gave in" she would want to be my girlfriend. Then she said that we were "just friends." Her hand was resting on my crotch at the same time, though. I told her that I also only wanted her to be my friend and that this was perfectly fine with me.

Having hung out a few hours together, we already developed some inside humour. For instance, whenever I teased her on her atrociously bad English she said she hated me. I said the same to her every time she teased me. "I hate you!", became a recurring theme, always followed by touching, playful slapping, hugging or kissing.

Two different guys kept texting and calling Skinny. One, Ego-Booster, she only used for validation, and she literally treated him like dirt. While she was cuddling up to me on a bench she received a text messages from him. She read it and shrugged. Twenty minutes of cuddling and making out later she said she should probably tell him that she won't show up for their date. While typing the text message she was in hysterics. Standards for text messaging are rather low anyway, but she wrote, "Sorry tomorrow OK." This roughly translates to, "Sorry for cancelling twenty minutes before our date. Is it OK if we meet tomorrow instead?" She did not even consider him worthy of a semi-decent text message.

The other guy bought her dinners and random things. Let's call him PROVIDER. I suggested she should use him to buy her stuff and that she could meet me afterwards for her other needs. He called repeatedly because she was late. Well, SKINNY was more than an hour late because of me. When she finally picked up the phone he told her he loved her. Such guys deserve to be used for their money.

While we were walking around the pond in the park she wanted to know the number of my ex-girlfriends, but I refused to tell her. This drove her mad. SKINNY pulled out her dictionary again. After some typing she asked me whether I was a "licentious man" and whether it was normal in Germany to have sex outside of relationships. Therefore I told her that people should be able to enjoy sex without the burden of a relationship if this is what they desire and that there was nothing wrong with it as long as both knew what to expect from each other.

"Do you only want me for one night?", she asked.

"I might want you for more than that."

Considering that she kept touching me it was a good answer. On our way back to the station she seemed to be really into me, touched me a lot, initiated hand-holding and rubbed my back. She did not want to come back to my place, though. I had told her that we could listen to some tunes, but she didn't like the idea. While we were walking down Oxford Street hand in hand, EGOBOOSTER called again. SKINNY gave him some real shit on the phone and aggressively told him off. I had a hard time keeping my chortling down.

At the crossroads Skinny gave me a passionate kiss. Some random drunk asshole interfered by shouting, "Put that thing away. You can get arrested for that!" I ignored him and dragged the girl off. After a few steps I gently pushed her against the wall and kissed her again. Unfortunately, this did not change her mind. She preferred to meet with Provider so that he could buy her some gifts. We parted after another passionate make out, only to never see each other again. It was a case of incompatible expectations.

Keep her horny and get her out of there!

On a Thursday night TERRY dropped me a text message, asking me whether I was up for going to Punk in Soho, one of the more fashionable clubs in London. Originally I wanted to stay in, but I changed my mind and decided to join him "for an hour or so."

Punk seemed to have lost its cool. It used to be packed to the brim with beautiful gay boys and a healthy selection of attractive young females, but not tonight. I almost felt uncomfortable because there were so many straight guys around. Really hot girls were few and far between. In the karaoke area I chatted up some girls. The first one was modestly interesting but she left to join her friends. The second one I considered pretty cool, mostly because she claimed to love Bukowski. On the looks scale, though, she was hardly more than a 7. This sadly made her one of the hotter girls that night. Her friend did not like me much and interfered. I did not really feel like fighting for that girl because I saw a tempting blonde in my vicinity. She got wet for me in no time, but another guy took over when I had left for a short moment. This is a typical risk of the trade.

TERRY and me considered leaving the venue early since we had the unpleasant feeling that we had already approached every desirable woman. I was slightly annoyed and commented to him, "Dude, I have not even kissed a girl tonight. This is completely unacceptable." But as I turned around I met the stare of OXFORD, a voluptuous blonde. I pulled her in. She seemed rather forward and tried to kiss me. I let her wait for about a minute. We just stood there, pressing our bodies against each other.

OXFORD ignored my suggestion to get some fresh air. The impression I got was that she only wanted to make out with me and nothing beyond that. Nonetheless, after my third or fourth attempt she followed me outside. We sat down, caressing each other and making out. It emerged that her flat was not only within walking distance but that we were actually living on opposite sides of the same street. After a while she complained that it was cold, so we went back inside.

Punk had a small room called *Dress-up Box* from which people could borrow clothes. This place was now unoccupied and unlit, which made it the perfect place to further amp up OXFORD. I sat her down on a sofa. My fingers wandered into her panties. Her pussy was nicely shaved, which earned her some more points in my book. She had a hard time holding herself back. I grabbed her hair, yanked her head back and hovered my lips about an inch from hers. Every time she wanted to come closer I yanked her head back a little bit more. Then I allowed her to get some gratification and made out with her while fondling her voluptuous body. But grabbing her ass and boobs was apparently a tad too steamy for this club. Someone slapped me on my shoulder. I looked up and saw a huge bouncer standing in front of us. He angrily yelled at me, "You can't do stuff like that in here, asshole!" Probably he was afraid I would fuck this girl right there. Considering that my cock was already in her hands, his concerns were legitimate.

After some minutes on the dance floor it was time to get some fresh air again. Despite all the hard work I had put into Oxford, she was not still not ready to be taken home. I tried regardless and led her off.

"Where are we going?", she asked.

"This way!"

"Where do you live?"

"Well, this way!"

It was clear to her what was up. She put up some resistance, so I told her I wanted to show her some "really bizarre music videos" on YouTube at my place. "Music videos on YouTube? How romantic!", she sarcastically retorted. I understood her comment as an agreement. Yet, she stopped. I looked deeply into her eyes and said I could walk her home tonight, which she answered with a submissive look and a breathed "maybe."

I was a bit too pushy afterwards. In the middle of our next make out she stopped me and said, "You know what, I think you should go home, and I should go back inside." Her tone of voice was neutral, so I had to treat carefully here. Because I am not much of a talker I gently pushed her against the wall and made out with her. Oxford arched her back and moaned. She was getting too much into it, so I stopped. We went back inside.

She probably needed a little bit more persuasion, so I grabbed her ass forcefully, put my other hand into her bra and played with her boobs. OXFORD responded very well to those actions but she tried to keep me on my toes as well. After I had teased but not kissed her she abruptly walked off with an annoyed look on her face and joined the crowd on the dance floor. I walked up to her again and continued with the treatment: hair pulling, ass grabbing, pressing her pussy against my thigh, you name it.

I playfully said to her that I reward good behaviour but that I also punish girls for bad behaviour. She turned around to grind her ass against my cock. After some moments she backed off and kept her distance for a bit, just to tease me. She came closer to whisper in my ears, "So, how are you going to punish me for this?" I took this as a call for drastic action and shoved my hand down her pants. While tonguing her down I fingered her. Then I abruptly walked off. She just stood there completely baffled. After she had processed what had happened she hurried after me and did not want to be separated from me anymore.

It was time to get out of the club but she had to go to the toilet first. After she came back we made out some more.

"Get your coat!", I told her.

"Oh.... Um.... I have to find my friend first."

I was under the impression that she was on her own. Her friend was one of her flatmates and she was reasonably good-looking as well. It seemed there was some kind of rivalry going on between them. The three of us left Punk together. I made sure to walk in between those two girls. The worst thing to happen would be if both got into a conversation I was excluded from, leaving me there standing there with my dick in my hands. But it all went well. OXFORD and me even ignored FLOORMATE for quite some time. She told me about some of her travel plans and some other things about her life.

Ten minutes later we were in front of her house. FloorMate walked in, but Oxford was hesitant. I firmly took her hand and opened the door. Her friend knew the deal apparently and quickly disappeared in the elevator. I stayed behind with Oxford. After some more light kissing I led her to the elevator as well. In her room things were straightforward. After a few minutes we were sitting on her bed and we quickly undressed each other. I pushed her into the pillows, got on top, teased her a bit by shaking my cock in front of her lips. She tried to get a hold of it, gasping for it like for fresh air. Eventually I did her the favour and shoved it into her mouth. Game over.

At Punk I thought Oxford was about average. Admittedly her sense of fashion was a bit odd, just like her boring haircut. However, lying next to me, after I was done with her, completely exhausted and with messed up hair, she looked amazing. Her naked body was just beautiful. It was a pleasant surprise.

There was no point in dropping a pretty girl that was literally living across the street. We kept seeing each other for a couple of weeks. However, during exam time I literally forgot about her. When I called her two weeks later she did not answer the phone anymore. It was no surprise. By the way, she got her name due to her father, a scientist at the University of Oxford.

Unexpected encounter at an upscale bar

I had become a regular at *Frat Party* at Ghetto, which was always quite a debauchery. It also was the only consistently good Monday night in London. However, I was not feeling it that night and went back outside. Looking for a change of scenery I roamed the streets and saw some people outside a venue I did not know yet. The bouncer told me it was £5 to get in, which I found relatively steep considering the day of the week. I told him that I bring the party and that it would thus be in his best interest to let me in for free. He did not believe me. A second bouncer joined our conversation and said he could take me to Club 49, where one of his buddies worked at the door. He told me he could get me in for free, but I am pretty sure he was bullshitting. It was probably free to enter anyway. I did not mind as I was excited for fate to lead me to a new place. Club 49 turned out to be a nice upscale bar.

Upon entering I spotted two jaw-dropping women, Great Ass and Long Hair. Both were leaning against the bar. They were in their late twenties, possibly early thirties, but, boy, were they hot: tall, trim, fake breasts, long hair. Now this was the level I wanted to play on! Because I was mentally still in club mode I hip-bumped Great Ass. She responded by slapping my ass. I returned the favour. After this short interaction she was already hooked and asked me the usual questions.

I did not tell her where I was from and said that she had to come up with something more original to keep my interest. Great Ass touched me just to see how I would react, but I did not react at all. Hence she turned around and gyrated her ass in front of me. Because I did not care about that either, she moved closer and rubbed her ass lightly against my groin. I was still not giving a fuck, so she put one of her hands behind her back and rubbed her thumb over my cock. I already had a hard-on because she was so incredulously sexy. She followed this up by fully grinding into me. It was impossible for me to restrain myself any longer, so I put my hands around her waist and pulled her in. Of course she immediately backed off.

I leaned against the bar, minding my own business. Actually, I was only curious to see what would happen. I gave off a disinterested vibe and the smirking grin on my face was more than just hinted at. Long Hair ordered a bottle of champagne and pulled out a wad of cash. She also ordered strawberries. Great Ass came back to me and again asked me where I was from (Berlin). This time I answered her question. Then she spoke to me in German. It was not flawless but I was impressed nonetheless. She was rubbing her firm ass against my cock and talking to me while looking over her shoulder to make eye contact. This was an uncomfortable position for her, but feeling my hard cock seemed to make it worth suffering for. Then she ate two strawberries in a highly suggestive manner while gazing deeply into my eyes. Afterwards she looked at me, slowly put her index finger in her mouth and bit it. She oozed sex. Of all the girls I had met so far she had by far the best game.

Great Ass walked off again. I thought it was just another one of her ploys, so I assumed my previous pose. After some moments she turned around.

"You are really persistent," she said.

"Huh?"

Now she got quite aggressive. She was just bullshitting, though

"Yeah, you are still right in my face."

"What are you talking about?"

She realised that she was hitting a brick wall. But because she wanted to continue the interaction, she had to try something else. She bit her finger again while looking me deep into my eyes. This was when I realised that it was in fact me who had hit a brick wall and was clueless. I did not know what to do and just stood there, desperately trying to look cool. Long Hair then pulled Great Ass away and both danced sexy to a Rihanna song in front of me for a while. After this was over, Long Hair took the bottle of champagne and walked off to a table. Her friend followed but looked back at me, which was an invitation to join them. I left the bar instead because I was too perplexed. This was too much for me to process. I was not yet at a level where I could crack cockteases of such a calibre.

"John, I'm only dancing."

Even though Exams were coming up, I could not resist going out. There was a huge party at Fabric in Farringdon. After two hours or so I was able to enjoy the mediocre music and the boring crowd. On the dance floor I spotted a girl with a truly impressive rack. I took her hand and led her away from her friends. We made out in no time. Then she received a text message and told me she would be "back in a sec."

I did not feel like wasting time any time and hit on the next girl as soon as she was out of sight. Fabric was really packed, so I only had to turn around and reach out for the most attractive girl in my vicinity: CURLY was tall, slim, had a perfect little ass and sweet perky breasts as well as an impressive mane of curly hair. She was dancing in a circle with some friends, so I mirrored her moves first. Within a minute she was grinding her pussy against my leg. It was time to get her away from her group. "I can't. I have to stay with my friends," she objected.

Standard procedure would be to befriend her friends and try again later, but the music was too loud. Another option was to make her forget everything around herself. I chose to do that.

We kissed for a bit, but I did not want her to get her hopes up too high and said that this would be all for now. She answered with a grin. When I suggested to "go somewhere else" she said she had to stay with her friends. Luckily they disappeared after a while.

I guided Curly's left hand over my body, under my shirt and then over my thighs. Then I put it on my crotch. As she was massaging my cock through my pants I whispered in her ear that there were so many things I would love to do with her. This put a huge smile on her face. Eventually I shoved her hand down my pants. Her fingers quickly found their way to my hard cock. This did not really do it for me, so I took a few steps back and leaned against the stage. She was rather horny and pressed her body against mine while playing with my schlong.

I put my hand in her pants and worked her tight ass. She was moaning. I was looking for a way to improve the situation. First I reached into my pants and made sure my dick was pointing upwards, which allowed her to work it better and stroke it properly. Curly was completely in trance and did not at all register what was going on around her anymore, not even a group of four girls to our right who excitedly tried to get a better look at the scene. Of course they did not dare to come too close. My jacket blocked the sight sufficiently anyway. There were people all around us and even behind us on stage, but nobody could really see what was going on. It was fairly obvious, though.

I pulled my cock halfway out and she stroked it more effectively. This went on for some minutes. Unfortunately her grip was a bit too loose and she was whacking it a tad too fast. I removed her hand. Although I only got close to busting a nut I got a surprisingly large amount of satisfaction out of it. For the record, the total time from initial meet to handjob was less than fifteen minutes and from what I could tell, CURLY was completely sober.

We danced some more and she was grinding and dry humping me like crazy. Yet, she still brought up that she was with some friends and therefore could not sit down with me somewhere. I did not see much room for progress. Eventually CURLY said she had to get back to her friends. I gave her a puppy look, which made her offer her number. However, there really was no point in following up with her. After she had left it struck me that I should have pulled down my pants a little bit and made sure my T-shirt covered my cock completely. This way she could have worked it properly. It was something to keep in mind for the future.

After the handjob intermezzo I spotted the girl with the truly impressive rack again. She was delighted to see me. I did not know whether she had witnessed what had happened between me and CURLY. We did the usual: kissing, grinding, dick rubbing, ass grabbing, tits squeezing. After a few moments, however, she got *another* call she had to answer. I let her go. There was no point in bothering with a girl that thought there was something more important to do than hooking up with me.

I was in an amazing mood and felt like I was walking on air. The next girl that caught my interest was FACE. Apart from her incredibly pretty face she was nothing special. She probably was still in her teens — and she gave me the same bullshit as CURLY, saying that she could not leave her friends. This did not bother me much, but then she pointed at her lips and said, "I have...." Unfortunately I could not understand the rest of the sentence because the music was too loud. It could have been cold sores or lipstick. Yet, the mere fact that she brought it up was enough to make me refrain from kissing her. There were no more make outs to be had for Face. I did not mind some more grinding and cock rubbing, though.

Face got increasingly turned on but she did not want to leave her friends, who were still dancing next to us. She tried to kiss me, but I did not let her, so she sucked on my neck instead. Suddenly Curly walked past, deliberately close to me. I gave her a high five and a big grin. This time she was alone, but I was a bit pissed at her because she was unwilling to leave her friends earlier. I ignored her and continued with Face.

Maybe I am a pervert, but as I was typing this story up, I got hard again. I clearly enjoyed Curly's public handjob more than bedroom sex. But maybe that's just me. When I checked her Facebook page, I not only found out that she and Big Hair had mutual friends but also that she had turned eighteen just two weeks prior, which explains her protectiveness. On all her pictures she looks sweet and innocent. Who would have guessed?

She bit me in less than two minutes

I did not feel like sitting at home and walked down the road to my favourite Monday night hangout Ghetto. The term was over and most students had left London for a couple of weeks. There were only lesbians there, which did not put me in the right mood for picking up girls. However, it was a great opportunity for toying around with a couple of recent ideas.

A suitable test object, TIGRESS, sat down right next to me. She did look like a lesbian, but her boobs were appealing. I gave her a bored look, which she answered with a smile. She moved her hands to the rhythm of the music, and I mirrored this for a while. Then I raised my right hand for a high five. After our fingers had interlocked I squeezed her hand and let her feel my strength. I stretched out my arm and kept it up in the air. She tried to get out of my grip.

People are usually impressed by my strength, especially considering that I am not that big. She was, too. I teased her with, "Come on, try to put your hand down. Just do it! … See, you can't." TIGRESS gave me an intrigued look that spelt, "What the fuck?" Then she asked me whether I was gay, which is girl-speak for, "You are handsome." I replied with a smirk. Then I put her arm around her neck and pulled her down to the sofa, so that she was lying beside me. I firmly looked into her eyes and said, "I can completely dominate you."

Tigress kept staring at me. And guess what she did next! Right, she bit me in my shoulder, really hard. This led to wrestling, which included mutual crotch-rubbing and ass squeezing. Of course I had to retaliate. We kept biting each other back and forth. I licked her face and neck, and she attempted to bite my fingers and everything else she could get a hold off. It was such a pleasure. (By the way, the marks she left on my body lasted several days.)

I thought this was enough and wanted her to cool down. She asked me where I was from. I let her guess and put my hand on her thighs, inching closer and closer to her pussy. She removed my hand shortly before reaching its destination and tried to bite me again. Then she told me she was from Sweden. Ah, Swedish girls! I have been lucky to meet my fair share of naughty girls from this country.

After rubbing her pussy for a while one of her friends eventually got curious and walked up to us. Tigress introduced me to her and I chatted with both for a while. I wasn't motivated to pull a girl that night but it was cool to hang out with those two.

The power of the penis

Putting people under a spell

I went to *Trailer Trash* at On The Rocks. The door policy is tough. It was cheap to get in, but not easy to get in, unlike so-called VIP clubs that charge ridiculously high cover of up to £20 for men while they are free for girls. In those places it is enough to dress nicely. On the other hand, On The Rocks has a system to repel the uninformed. There were two queues, one for the guest list and a regular one. However, there never was a guest list. Those in the know queue for the guest list and get shooed in, whereas more plain-looking guys might queue there but eventually get sent away or told to join the other queue.

The people running these club nights have different standards. Pussy means nothing to them because for the most part it's a gay scene anyway. I have seen groups of breathtaking Scandinavian teenage girls getting turned away because their overly revealing Leicester Square outfit was not appreciated. All that mattered were appearances and meeting certain criteria. The regular queue had easily over one hundred people, all eagerly waiting to get in. Those people had to wait more than an hour while I walked right in. I even got a concession without having to show my student ID.

A girl was walking around the club, collecting email addresses of people she found interesting. I had been to *Trailer Trash* a couple of times before, but had not yet reached the upper echelons. She walked up to me. “I was wondering whether we could take your email address so that we could send you special information or announcements from time to time,” she said. I replied, “Why don’t you let me write it down? I’d like to have some control over the process.” Afterwards I hustled her into kissing me on the cheek. Out of curiosity I kept an eye on her for a few minutes and indeed she barely approached any people. I felt special.

Two other girls with rather expensive-looking cameras were taking pictures for a blog on fashion. They claimed it was one of the largest of its kind and that they were travelling the world to follow current trends. I did not bother to remember the name of the blog because I don’t particularly care about such matters. The instant they saw me they both got excited and wanted to take pictures of me. They also requested me to dance for a bit on my own to shoot this as well.

Afterwards those girls dragged me around the club, ordering other girls to dance with me or putting groups of interesting looking people together. Then they told another girl to dance with me. She was very responsive to my touch but I quickly dropped her because her looks did not quite match her stellar outfit.

Seven girls, six make outs

There was a girl that was part of the entourage of the fashion bloggers. After they were done taking pictures of me, she ran up to me and squeaked, "I love you!" Then she gave me an intense hug. We made out for a bit afterwards but I let her go because I was not especially interested in her. Girls used to get annoyed when I kissed them but left soon afterwards. With my easy-going "I take what I want" rockstar attitude this seemingly was no longer a problem. I could literally walk up to girls, make out with them and return for more later, sometimes even after making out with another girl right in front of them.

On the dance floor I spotted Locks. I offered her a high five but didn't let go of her hand afterwards. She asked me whether I was French, a question I regularly get. My standard reply is, "I know that I'm really good-looking, so thanks for the compliment." She was not used to such cocksure responses, which made her even wetter for me. A guy was hovering around her. I suspected it was her boyfriend, which she confirmed. Since I was after either instant gratification in the club or pulling a girl home, I decided to let her go. She was really pretty, though. Her boyfriend still had his back turned to her, so I put two fingers on her cheek, turned her head and went in for another make out. Locks was visibly impressed by such a display of boldness. Boyfriends had become a non-issue for me.

I have repeatedly tried to force myself to get at least the contact details from girls that show some interest but can't go all the way for whatever reason. Locks was clearly into me, so a future meet-up might well have been in the cards. Yet, I always found it quite bothersome to meet girls for dates in London — public transport was a mess.

A little bit later I spotted Bites, took her hand, pulled her in, and made out with her. I had had so many instant make outs recently that it already felt completely natural even though it was utterly ridiculous. We had great sexual chemistry. Interestingly enough, I initially thought that I would take her home, which was not bad for a sixth sense. However, our initial encounter did not end too well. She left after a few minutes, which I found a bit strange. Maybe she was only playing hard to get.

The forth girl I met was the hottest in the venue: blonde, skinny, great rack, but she was also a bit trashed. In honour of the colour of her tight dress I shall call her Pink. She loved me. Things were becoming somewhat repetitive: I pulled her in and tongued her down. She was very aggressive and took the next step by dragging me off to a quieter area, which took me by surprise. "Do I know you?", she asked me in a sincere tone. I said she did, which was not exactly true. She did not seem to mind and we continued making out while feeling each other up. Then we went back outside, where she told me about her job interview the next morning. It was for the position of personal assistant for a rather conservative company and she mocked the whole process. With a faux posh accent she spouted out a few standard telephone phrases such as, "Can I take your name and number?", while squeezing one of her boobs and giving me a rather horny look. Her smile lingered.

Pink was more than just a bit tipsy. The problem in such cases is that the girl's friends have a tendency to become extremely protective because they don't want their friend to make a "mistake." Obviously, without such guardianship she would just do what she wanted and needed. You would not believe the level of resistance you sometimes get. Her friends did not push me away or insulted me, things that happened to me in other places, but one of those guys tried to pull a dirty trick nonetheless. "Hey you, give him my number!", PINK shouted at him. He opened the contact register in his phone and gave me a random number, but on the display I could clearly read that it wasn't PINK's name. I wasn't having any of it. "PINK, give me your phone. He apparently has the wrong number," I shouted over to her.

I keyed my number into her phone and called it. At the same time she was grinding her ass against my cock, which was one of my favourite positions when talking to a woman. She turned her head around and said, "Call me — I love you!" After passionately kissing me on my cheek she ground her ass harder against my groin. I rubbed her labia through her dress and she was getting really into it. Funnily enough, when I put my middle finger down her ass crack she panicked and shouted, "No thumb!" For some reason this got me really hard. It also gave me some inspiration for future endeavours. Unfortunately PINK had to leave because of her job interview, which was a shame as she was clearly down to fuck.

LOCKS reappeared. She ran up to me while shouting, "AARON, AARON!" This time she was with a really classy-looking girlfriend. I hugged LOCKS before I turned to CLASSY. The moment I laid eyes on her she got the deer in headlights look. As if in a trance she put her hand on my belly and read out loud the print on my pink T-shirt. It said, "Lick. Suck. Bite." Afterwards she put on what must have been her most seductive smile and placed a gentle kiss on every single word. As soon as she had finished, I grabbed her neck, pulled her in and made out with her. After a while she stopped me and said she had to return to her boyfriend. LOCKS found this quite funny and said, "This is the exact same thing that happened before!" Instead, she should have said that this was exactly the same thing I *had done* before. However, to girls things always "just happen."

The night was already ridiculous. I felt like a rockstar. I did not even actively look for girls anymore but merely walked around the club, having fun and entertaining myself. Whenever I saw an interesting girl, I did something playful with her. GREAT WALL was next in line. She was actually from Australia, but from Chinese ancestry. I high-fived her and pulled her a little bit closer. Then she reached for her glass which was almost empty, but full of ice cubes. She told me she liked to lick on cold ice cubes, and took two small ones into her mouth. I wanted to have one of them, pulled her close and went for the kiss. A make out ensued. Too bad she did not get my idea. I wanted her to pass me one of the ice cubes with her tongue but she quickly swallowed them.

GREAT WALL was not the most appealing girl around but definitely doable. In order to persuade her of what an amazing guy I was I shoved her hand down my pants. She resisted at first but then nonetheless put her thumb deep into my underpants and rubbed my skin. This was also quite a turn on. It was time to take this interaction somewhere else, so I dragged her outside. "Are we going for a smoke?", she asked me. "Sure."

She told me that she was about to visit Berlin and asked me whether I could give her some hints. This was too much conversation for my taste already, so I changed the pace. "Touch my cock!", I told her. She smiled, but did not comply. I looked deeply into her eyes and said, "Come on!" Because she still did not do it, I put her hand on my crotch. She let it rest there, but moments later we were passionately making out while she was rhythmically rubbing my crotch. However, when I tried to shove her hand down my pants she objected and said with a lovely smile, "You have to let me do it on my own pace. Is it okay for you to wait one or two more hours?"

After we went back inside, she got sidetracked by her group. She was with two friends, a guy and a girl, who both did not approve of me. Otherwise it would have been a done deal. The male in the group had mustered up enough courage to make a move and went for the kiss. It was a half-arsed attempt, though. Upon noticing me he asked her who I was. When she told him he exchanged glances with the other girl and dragged GREAT WALL off. "I am sorry, but we have to leave," she said while her friends were leading her to the exit. They did not leave her a choice, which I found fairly aggressive. The night was far from over, though.

LONG-TERM was a blonde girl I tried to warm up slowly. On three occasions I hip-bumped, spun her around or high-fived her. It seemed to have worked because she was quite friendly when I finally attempted a full-on physical approach. She was not an instant make out candidate, though. Overall, she was a bit too frigid, but I could sense that she liked me. We were dancing next to each other for a while, before she walked away. She turned around and said, "We are going for a smoke!" I took this as an invitation to follow her group outside.

Outside, however, a cute Australian girl suddenly stood next to us. I asked her, "You look a bit confused. What's the matter?" AUSSIE revealed that she had sneaked into On The Rocks without paying, while her friends were still waiting outside. I playfully accused her of being a vile and immoral person. She laughed and told me bits of her biography. At the same time I was palming her ass. Unfortunately she did not want to make out with me. This was fine because she was already reasonably aroused. I only had to gradually turn things more sexual. "I think I'll wait outside for my friends. You don't have to stay with me if you don't want to," she said. It was clear that she was suffering from low self-esteem, which was an impression I already had from her rather timid body language. "I have a better idea. Why don't you come with me to dance?", I responded.

I took her hand and led her back inside. Her grip was firm and she pumped my hand repeatedly. She offered to buy me a drink. I like girls who know that they are hot and act accordingly. But this girl was hot and insecure. She would not have needed to bribe me with a drink, although I appreciated the gesture. She left for a moment to talk to a friend and I decided to dance by myself for a bit. Then I bumped into Bites again and reengaged her. This really pissed off Aussie. As she walked past she looked right through me. It was unfortunate that she had not been more cooperative because she could have enjoyed my company for the night.

Cock out on the dance floor

I quicky made out again with Bites. It was still on. I put her hand on my crotch, but she was reluctant. After some more make outs, though, she let it rest there but did not make much of an effort to get me hard. I put my hand on hers and rubbed it over my crotch. At last she got the hint, but this was not good enough for me. But when I tried to shove her hand down my pants I encountered more resistance. I pulled my trousers down and my cock out. When I put her hand on it again, she got to work. No girl can resist touching a nice warm hard cock. First she worked the head, then I guided her hand to stroke the whole shaft. In combination with more passionate make outs this was quite an enjoyable experience.

After she had whacked my cock for a while I dragged her outside because I wanted her to get to know me better. This was where we *started* the actual conversation. She introduced herself. "I'm pleased to meet you, Bites. I have a feeling we will get along really well," I replied in a completely serious tone. This cracked her up. It turned out that we had quite a few things in common. We had a good connection and her rubbing the tip of my cock while pressing her body against mine made our conversation stimulating on another level as well.

She did not seem to have a problem with stroking my rod in public, so I tried to get more out of the situation. First I guided her hand to move faster, which led to more intense cock rubbing and make outs. "Now get down on your knees and lick it!", I ordered her. "No, I can't do that," she replied while giggling. It was worth a try. Admittedly, it would have greatly surprised me if she had gone down on me in front of about dozen people. On the other hand, at On The Rocks I have seen people snorting coke in the open, so morals were definitely a bit on the loose side. We chatted some more. Eventually she dropped that she had to go home soon. "Sure, just get your coat and let's get out of here," I said.

Bites told me she usually doesn't do "things like this," but I suggested that we could just "chill" at her place and that we wouldn't have to do anything. She raised no further objections, but she wanted to inform her two gay friends first. She said goodbye to them and then we went back to her place. Amusingly enough she rationalised her taking me home with the fact that I lived quite far away and that it would have taken me about an hour to get back home. Of course she could not let such a horrible thing happen.

Bites was fairly cool and she was the first girl I had a genuine fuck buddy relationship with. After a couple of weeks she got a bit too needy for my taste, so I ended it. But we definitely had a lot of fun together. The belt I borrowed from her is a keepsake that still reminds me of her, and it made many girls compliment me on my style. Sorry, Bites, for never returning it. I just could not part from such a cool accessory.

From one flower to the next

After a wild night with BITES and less than two hours of sleep it would have been wiser to stay in. However, I went to *After Skool Club* at The Quad instead. This used to be a somewhat boring night and I expected to stand out quite a bit. I hadn't been to this place for about a year and was thus surprised that the crowd was quite fashionable. It was not at all like I remembered it.

Two tanned blonde girls caught my attention. I walked up to the first one and spun her around. In her heels she was about six feet tall, so I told her I almost felt intimidated by her height. She was a bit thick or very insecure, or maybe she just could not process what was happening because she kept staring at me with her eyes wide open, unable to form a coherent sentence. I could not bring myself to continue with her. However, her friend PLATINUM BLONDE was not too bad either. I did the usual: spin, pull in, make out. She said something I could not quite hear. Her feeble voice really annoyed me. She tried again. "You must have a girlfriend!", she squeaked. "Yeah. Actually, I've got a couple."

PLATINUM BLONDE was lost for words. Either she had no sense

of humour or she viewed me as the epitome of a player. On the other hand, Bites went nuts the night before and left about a dozen hickeys on my neck which my scarf did not hide too well. She pointed to her friend and said to me, "Well, this is *my* girlfriend!" I pulled her in again and we danced close for a while. Unfortunately she did not know how to move. I quickly got bored of her and decided to ditch her. However, I wanted to make out with her some more first. Platinum Blonde did not seem to like this idea. I told her I was about to leave and pointed two fingers at my cheek, which she kissed. Then I put my index finger on my lips. She pointed her finger in a direction far away and said, "But only if you go this way!" This yielded another make out, but she wasn't worth any further effort.

To my great surprise I ran into Big Hair again. She still seemed to like me. One of Big Hair's friends had given me a call early in the morning, telling me that she had described me as "buff and really indie looking." Her friends viewed me as pretty cool and did not seem to mind that I was a huge slut. Some of them have repeatedly seen me making out with random girls or rubbing their crotch. I was not especially interested in Big Hair anymore, but we made out for a bit nonetheless. After a few moments I left her because I wanted to pursue the unknown.

I was leaning against a pillar and looking around bored. Tipsy danced in front of me and tried to get my attention. After a while I pulled her in and made out with her. She was certainly not wasted, but her kisses tasted of alcohol. Before I could say anything to her I spotted Pixie and quickly let go of Tipsy. Pixie was only about five feet tall and incredibly petite. We made eye contact while she was dancing next to me. I told her to put her phone away, which she held in one of her hands, so that we could dance properly. After two or three minutes

I pulled her in to give her a hug and she rubbed my back intensely. I lifted her up and made out with her. We continued our dance. Then I dragged her off. Luckily, there were some very comfortable seats scattered around the area. I sat down and pulled her on my lap.

While caressing each other and making out we chatted for a while. Pixie claimed to have friends staying at her place, which limited my options. She struck me as a cool girl and she was incredibly sexy. Thus I preferred to stick with her instead of chasing after other girls. She repeatedly said she had to get back to her friends, but whenever she got up I looked into her eyes and told her to sit down on my lap again.

"So, why do you like me so much?", I asked her.

"I love your accent."

This was utter nonsense because we had only exchanged a few sentences. I paused and smiled.

"And what else?"

"Well, you are this tall and dark-haired mysterious stranger. I really like that."

She played with my hair and got more and more into me. The sofa next to us was now free, so we moved over there. I lied down, put her on top of me and worked her ass. My hand was already in her pants. Eventually I thoroughly fingered her from behind. Big Hair and her entourage witnessed all of this. Seeing Pixie writhing on my lap seemed to have mildly amused them. I felt amazing as always and I loved how she tried to suppress her orgasms. Pixie left shortly before the club closed to finally get back to her friends. I'm sure I had made her night. She certainly had made mine.

I had gotten a significant boost for my ego, not that I had needed one, and was willing to call it a night. On my way to the exit I remembered Tipsy and decided to hunt her down. She was dancing at the other end of the dance floor, close to the stage. I walked up to her, pushed her against the stage and did *not* kiss her. Instead I put my thumb on her forehead, my fingers on her cheek and slowly moved my hand downward. Eventually I stuck my thumb in her mouth and let her suck on it for a while, before I made out with her. I barely talked to her at all, but she said a few nice things like calling me brilliant and sexilicious. At least I learnt a new word that night. I put her hand on my crotch and she rubbed it. Then I made out with her again, before I gently pushed her away. She took this as a cue to play hard to get and walked off. After a while I went looking for her and found her in the other room sitting all by herself, with a glass of beer in her hand. I grabbed a chair and sat down next to her.

"Do you know The Roxy?", she asked me.

"Yeah, I do. But it's a bit boring there, isn't it?"

"I go there every Tuesday."

She told me more about herself. One of her friends joined us. He was a really cool guy so it was not difficult to befriend him. Soon afterwards he walked off. Now Tipsy dropped a bomb: "I advise you to find your friends now. Otherwise, you will be stuck with me for the rest of the night." This is not a bad way for a girl to say that she is craving for your cock.

The lights went on. I took Tipsy's hand and wanted to drag her outside. She realised she had not collected her coat yet. Unfortunately she had not left it at the cloakroom but stuffed it under one of the sofas instead — and now she couldn't find it anymore. I watched her panicking for a while. Because she couldn't get a grip on herself I decided to go home alone. In this state she would have been far too much trouble.

Out of curiosity I checked Pixie's Facebook page. She was in a relationship, which amused me. Looking back, I have not the slightest doubt that I could have gotten her into a bathroom stall.

No, I'm not a doctor

I had been to two clubs already and was bored out of my mind. A third club, The Roxy, was close by. However, it was around 2 a.m. already. I found it unwise to blow money on cover charge and decided to head home instead. As I was walking past, someone yelled, "Aaron! It's Aaron!" It was one of Big Hair's gay friends. He stood there with one of his female friends, one I had been introduced to some nights ago. Big Hair had apparently showed him my MySpace profile, which included some seminude pictures of mine.

"We've seen your pictures on MySpace. Can I have a look at your nipples?", he asked.

"Say what?"

His hand was already under my T-shirt and he tried to lift it up. I calmly took his hand away.

"Oh, come on, Aaron. You are so sexy. Please let me see your chest!", he implored me.

"Forget it."

The girl decided to chime in.

"Well, you can have a look at my tits if you let me see your chest."

This was not bad for a reaction from a virtual stranger. She pulled her top down and exposed her right boob. It was a pretty nice one, so I played with it for a moment before she put it away.

"OK. Now let me touch your hairy chest!"

She put her hand under my shirt, rubbed my chest and said, "Mmmm…."

The gay guy apparently found this a bit strange, so he cock-blocked me and said, "Oh my God, AARON, you are so sexy. But we have to go inside again." Then he dragged this horny young girl back inside the venue. What a twat!

“Come on, show me your cock!”

While I was strolling around in the East End area, two young girls asked me for the way. Both were quite good-looking and because we were going in the same direction they joined me. I held hands with the more attractive one for a few moments and asked her what she was carrying around in her bag. She stopped to show me a dress she had bought at a Stella McCartney sample sale that day and proudly concluded her little speech on why she had to buy it with “...and it nicely accentuates my breasts. It might look like nothing as it is, but on me looks really great.” Admittedly, she did have a fantastic rack. However, since she was only trying to bait me to comment on her boobs, I ignored her statement.

We walked together for a while, then we arrived at The Aquarium. I should have joined those two girls, but I did not know that they were the hottest I would see that night. STELLA would have been up for at least a quick make out. Unfortunately her brother showed up out of nowhere, so instead of tonguing her down we only hugged and exchanged kisses on the cheek. The Aquarium was dead, so I went back outside, only to bump into

Stella and her friend again a little bit later. I was still determined to find a good club so I did not make use of the second opportunity of joining them for a drink at The Old Blue Last.

After I had bored myself to death in some bars and small clubs I walked back to The Aquarium. It was a cock farm like no other. A girl was taking pictures for a website and wanted to take some of me as well. I found her to be quite flirty and after a high five we wrestled for a bit. She was quite good-looking, but because she was there to work I had to look elsewhere for entertainment.

On the dance floor I spotted Dancer, a cute little girl in a revealing black dress. We danced for a while, then we sat down on a nearby sofa. Our conversation was fairly pointless, but it emerged that she was leaving London in two days and temporarily staying with friends. Going to her place was thus no option. The next day she had to take care of a couple of things, which meant that she could not sleep over at my place either.

Dancer said she was meeting up with a guy who was "sort of" her boyfriend the next day. Still, it did not take long until her hands were all over my body. Mine were squeezing her tits and running over her pussy. Moments later we were making out heavily. We went outside because it was hard to have a conversation to booming techno music. She told me more about her studies of modern dance and showed me some interesting moves as well as elements from a style called contact improvisation. The vibe was fairly sexual.

I put my hand inside her bra and played with her stiff nipples while talking about some random things. Dancer seemed to like this a lot. Earlier she had told me some crap that there had to be a "common level of spirituality" for her in order to be intimate with someone. I said she should just enjoy herself and cherish the moment. When I guided her hand down my pants, however, she objected and said she did not need "another dick" in her life. I retorted that my big warm hard cock would feel great in her hands nonetheless and that she would enjoy wrapping her fingers around it. She looked at me for a prolonged moment and blushed. Then she blurted out that my body was "so beautiful." She was sold. The only remaining question was whether I could get some action.

I ordered her to touch my cock and added, "It's beautiful, and you know you want to." She ate it up. "You seem to be really eager to show me your cock. So show it to me!", she demanded. But as I wanted to pull my pants down, she stopped me with, "No, not here. Let's go somewhere else." The cloak room area came to my mind first, but she objected that there were too many people. Personally, I do not care too much about such things. The attendant in the male toilet held her back when I walked toward the stalls, and upon entering the ladies' toilet we created a huge spectacle. All the girls were staring at me. One walked past with a seductive smile and rubbed my crotch for a moment. Then she looked back at me. I probably should have ditched DANCER for her. The female attendant said that she couldn't let me in. Another girl walked up to us and addressed the attendant with, "That's okay. He is a gentleman!" Maybe she was being ironic.

We had to look elsewhere. I told DANCER to get a wristband for re-entry and we left the club. Outside we quickly found a semi-secluded spot in a parking area. She was pretty eager and blurted out, "Okay, now show me your cock!" I pulled it out and whacked it. It got bigger, and so did her eyes. "That's very nice!", she said while staring at my pecker. With her finger tips she tickled my balls and with her palms she rubbed my cock for a bit. "You should see it when it is fully erect!", I said. "Okay!" However, not only did my dick grow. Her level of discomfort grew as well. After all, it was around 4.30 a.m. and the sun had already risen. It was more or less broad daylight. She backed off. "You could help yourself and I'll wait around the corner until you're done," she said. "Why don't you give me a hand?" I put my cock once again into her palms, but she did not feel like it. I think with a bit more time I would have been able to blow a load of jizz on her. She probably feared that something like this would happen and urged me to go back to The Aquarium. Inside, we cuddled and kissed some more and eventually parted at the end of the night. I took her number just for the sake of it, but there was no point to it since she was leaving London soon.

Like a point-and-click adventure game

At 1 a.m. I left Ghetto, bored out of my mind. Mondays were always a bit slow, but there was nothing at all to chose from at this club. In my rockstar swagger I spotted a cute girl outside a bar. She gave me an intrigued look. I walked right up to her, but she was quicker than me and asked, "Do you know where I could get some ganja?" I ignored what she said, took her hand and spun her around. To be honest, I did not even know what ganja was. "What was that?", I asked.

Ganja repeated her question. I told her that since she was already drinking she shouldn't need weed on top of that. We still held hands and I pulled her in closely. I turned her head and made out with her. She was hooked and pressed her body against mine. One of her hands was on my chest, and she complimented my sense of fashion. "I thought you were gay," she said. I smiled and asked her whether she still thought so. She hugged me intensely and would not let go of me. Of course, one of her friends had to pull her away. I walked off as I had yet to process what I had just done.

In the area around Tottenham Court Road station I noticed 101, a mainstream bar. In all these months in London I had only walked past it, but I was bored already and it couldn't get much worse. There was a fine blonde girl on the dance floor. I took her hand and pulled her in.

"I'm sorry, but I have a boyfriend," she protested.

"Don't worry, I am gay."

Her boyfriend really was in the venue, but I felt lucky and stuck with her regardless. Excitedly she turned to her female friend and said, "This is my new best gay friend!" She loved me. Of course she did. However, she was not stupid and soon realised that I probably was not gay after all. I think she noticed my boner. With a sceptical look on her face she asked me, "Are you sure you are gay?" Because I don't like to lie I ignored her question. We chatted for a while, before the interaction fizzled out and I left the bar.

Near Soho Square I ran into GANJA again. She was with a female friend, the one that had interfered earlier, and a rather aggressive guy. I'll call him AGGRO. GANJA was visibly delighted to see me. Her two friends seemingly had an argument. AGGRO had met her friend, but she was not willing to come home with him. He tried to persuade her, apparently in vain. Not that I really cared about it.

Something stuck out of GANJA's pocket, so I pulled it out. It was a wrapped brownie, and she offered it to me. AGGRO walked up to us and argued with the girl. Eventually he asked me whether I really wanted to have the brownie. I said I would. He gave me a long hard look and said I should just keep it. He was visibly annoyed and walked off again.

"Is he your boyfriend?", I asked GANJA. "Heaven forbid. He's just a friend. ... He just doesn't get it." She looked at me with her eyes wide open and said, "But you, you're not like him. You're really ahead of the game." I am, but she had no idea who she was dealing with. Another guy walked past. GANJA asked him for a cigarette, which he interpreted as an invitation to join us. It turned out that CIGARETTE GUY was pretty cool. GANJA had to talk to the other girl and I did not mind some company. AGGRO turned around. "Do we now have a fucking audience or what?", he shouted. We collectively ignored him. He came close to me and CIGARETTE GUY. Upon realising that we really did not give a fuck about him, he tried to befriend us and opened up his heart. "I really don't get women," he confessed. CIGARETTE GUY offered some condolence.

"How old are you?", he asked.

"I'm twenty-five."

"You're twenty-five — and you still haven't figured out women?"

He said it in a very calm and slow tone of voice. AGGRO was confused and walked off. CIGARETTE GUY shrugged. He pulled out a pack of cigarettes and offered me one as well. Even though I didn't smoke, I took it anyway because you never know.

The group of three had to leave. I pulled GANJA in again and made out with her some more. "Do you want to hang out some time?", I asked her. She said, "Sure!", and keyed her number into my phone. Afterwards I talked to CIGARETTE GUY some more. For a moment I thought about getting his contact details as well, but I was leaving the U.K. soon anyway.

It was past 2 a.m. Back at the crossroads at Tottenham Court Road station I bumped into a group of Spanish tourists. Spanish girls were among my favourites, so I was delighted. One of the girls asked me for the directions to Ghetto, the place I found so boring earlier that night. I spun her around, which I transitioned into hand holding. While I was embracing her I told the group that I would take them to this club. Then I tried to kiss this girl right there in the street, but she refused my advances. My intention was thus to amp her up at the club.

We walked to the club, holding hands. Ghetto was closing in about thirty minutes so we walked in free of charge. She asked where the cloak room was. As she wanted to walk off with her friends I held her back, led her around the corner, pushed her against the wall and tongued her down. She completely got into it. Her problem was that she was uncomfortable with showing affection in front of her friends. When she returned from the cloak room I realised that she did look much better with her jacket on. I immediately lost my interest. For a moment I considered continuing with her petite female friend who I was already grinding with. But something else was more enticing, incidentally another Spanish girl. I am not the biggest fan of the looks scale, but if asked I would rate her at least a 9.5.

This girl blew me away. As soon as I had seen her I went after her. She was a truly amazing kisser and the best I had enjoyed in a while. Did I mention that she was skinny, tall, and endowed with a perfect ass and great breasts? After about two songs I dragged her outside. She wanted to go back to her friends to get a cigarette, but I had one in my back pocket. It emerged that she was a tourist, sharing a room with her friend.

The most amusing part of the interaction was her reply to my statement that she was a really good kisser: "Yes, Spaniards are the best kissers. Then come Italians, French, and Portuguese." This was an interesting way to confess that she was not only quite conceited but also that she had rather loose morals. She would have been great material. I took her number and left. Of course, it was worthless, but it was a great fifteen-minute interaction nonetheless.

The night was not yet over. As I sat down on the night bus, I noticed a black girl behind me and turned around. Her face looked quite nice, so I offered her my brownie. She took it. We chatted for a bit, then I sat down next to her. She immediately pressed her thighs against mine. Unfortunately, she was from East London and I had severe problems with her accent. I couldn't be arsed to put much effort into it, but she provided some entertainment on my way home. She repeatedly asked me whether I was drunk. Apparently it was inconceivable for her that someone could be sober and talk to girls.

Some of my friends have remarked that the brownie was most likely a hash brownie. Thus it was no surprise that AGGRO got upset when GANJA wanted to give it to me. He wanted to keep it for themselves. I was completely unaware of this possibility because I don't do drugs. Let's hope the black girl did not get into any kind of trouble because of it. Anyway, playing LucasArts adventures on the PC certainly never was as much fun as that night.

In-venue insanities

Attempting to steal a girl's pants, and more

My buddy Cosy had recently challenged me to get a girl's pants. I did not want to wreck my chances with the really attractive girls, so I decided to only try this if a girl was less desirable. On the other hand I usually only hit on girls I consider hot, which made this challenge quite difficult. But sometimes girls feel lucky and they approach me.

As I was leaning against the stage at KOKO in Camden the girl next to me gave me an intrigued look. Her face was pleasant to look at, but her body was not. I pulled her in and put my forehead against hers. She quickly got into me. I gave in and kissed her on the lips, but only for the sake of Cosy's challenge.

"You know what, I'd really like to get your pants," I said.

"Huh?"

"Would you mind taking off your pants for me?"

"It's a bit crowded in here, isn't it?"

"Then let's go somewhere else."

I took her hand and tried to walk off with her, but she freaked out and left. It made me laugh.

As I looked around I spotted a blonde with ginormous knockers. She was very slim, which made her look like a comic figure. Too bad some other guy was quicker to approach. He tongued her down within a minute or so. This girl definitely wanted to hook up. But maybe they had known each other before. Whatever, you never know if you don't bother to find out. She made eye contact with me a couple of times throughout the night, though.

A reasonably good-looking girl was on the dance floor. She wore hot pants and a top that constantly slipped down. This exposed her bra, but Loose Top did not seem to particularly mind. We danced for a while in a very physically demanding manner and she tremendously enjoyed it. A random guy walked up to me.

"No offence, buddy, but she's got a boyfriend," he said.

"So what?"

"Nothing. I'm just telling you."

"Do you think I really care whether she's got a boyfriend or not?"

This wanker did not have the balls to make a move himself and now that he saw me getting Loose Top excited he wanted to talk me out of it. One of her female friends, however, was a bit concerned and pulled her away from me. I let her go.

I scoped out KOKO for a while but did not find anything of particular interest. After about twenty minutes I returned to

Loose Top and continued where we had left off. After some grinding I put her hand on my crotch and she enthusiastically rubbed it. She turned around and gyrated her ass forcefully against my cock. However, when I tried to shove her hand down my pants she did not play along. "You are really naughty, aren't you?", she said as she turned her head around — and slid her fingers in for about an inch.

Loose Top definitely put more effort into turning me on afterwards. I have no idea how far I could have taken this interaction because I noticed Angel, an unusually attractive Asian girl. I immediately let go of the other girl and walked over to her. We mirrored each other's movements for a while before we engaged in dancing. She made some witty remarks like the following.

"I bet you aren't a vegetarian!"

"Why is this important?"

"Because I only kiss vegetarians. I've tried to kiss non-vegetarians, but it just doesn't work for me."

"I haven't eaten meat today, so you shouldn't have a problem with that."

She giggled. My statement was only technically true, though, because it was past midnight. Being a big boy I try to have some poultry or fish every day.

"But I bet you don't do Yoga," she continued.

"I do. I practise Ashtanga."

"No, you don't!"

"Yes, I do."

"No way! I only kiss guys who do Yoga, because the others aren't worth it — and I don't want to kiss you because I don't know you."

Those were probably the most intelligent words a girl has ever used to tell me she fancied me. Then she made the so-called dancer pose, which is one of the balance positions in Yoga. I responded with the tree pose. We erupted in laughter.

The vibe was getting increasingly sexual. After some mutual ass grabbing I put one of her hands on my six-pack.

"This isn't normal!", she cooed.

"I know it's amazing. Just enjoy it."

She seemed fairly into me, so I suggested to go somewhere else and dragged her off. We sat down on a sofa and I pulled her down on my lap. ANGEL was pretty amazing and she had her life together as well. I couldn't say the same about myself. By the way, she worked as a model agent. Judging from her looks she may well have been a model herself earlier in her life. Her face was very beautiful and perfectly symmetrical. She was now in her late twenties. However, I wasn't really looking for a girlfriend, and building as well as maintaining a social circle in London would have been a Herculean task, so I did not even bother to get her contact details.

The main problem I had with ANGEL was that she seemed to be quite out of touch with her sexuality. For instance she said, "Don't look into my eyes. I promise you'll fall in love with me." However, she said it the way a little girl would say it. There was no doubt that she was very intelligent, but that alone did not do it for me. Yet, I was most impressed when she blurted out, "I bet you take your clothes off for a living!" This was partly true since I was doing live modelling.

Unfortunately her kisses lacked passion. Heck, there was no passion at all in them. It was interesting to talk to her, but after a while I did not feel a sexual vibe anymore. She wanted to rejoin her friends and I tagged along.

Pleasing an asian beauty in front of an audience

Angel ignored me as soon as I had rejoined her group. Yet, I was not in the mood to walk off because Devil, one of her two female friends, looked pretty damn amazing: big eyes, full lips, slim frame but massive breasts. I took her hand and pulled her in. She was a bundle of exuberant sexual energy. Of course, since she had seen me walking off with Angel earlier I could not go for the make out right there. Yet, we were hot for each other in no time. The teasing was great. We respectively went in for the kiss a number of times but always stopped shortly before reaching each other's lips. Her grinding was good, too.

"Let's take a break!", I said and dragged her off to sit down at a nearby sofa in a corner, where I pulled her down in my lap. She was all over me in an instant. We were heavily making out while fondling each other. Devil wore a short silk dress, which made it easy to rub her clit through her panties. Those were already soaked through, so I couldn't resist sliding my middle finger in. Her pussy was wet and warm and it felt so good!

The obvious next step would be to pull my cock out — and I did it! Devil was stroking me while tonguing me down. I wore a long scarf to cover hickeys from a previous adventure, which I only had to let down to cover up the movement of her hands.

This setup was just perfect. (After that night I barely ever went out without a scarf again.) "We better go somewhere else," I said.

We went into the next room. I pushed her against the wall outside the men's toilet and gave her a better taste of my fingering skills, before fully pulling my cock out again. I switched positions so that I could lean against the wall while DEVIL was pressing her body against mine. Thankfully this spot was quite secluded. She proceeded to whack me off and did not hold herself back at all. I love passionate women. It did not really matter anymore what I said as she was too much into me already.

"You've got the most beautiful breasts," I told her.

"Do you think so? I think they're a bit too small."

"They are perfect."

I gave them a squeeze while accusing her of turning me on so much so that I could not help but go after her the way I did. She certainly enjoyed the kind of attention she received. Too bad I could not get her to come into the men's room with me. She stopped me with:

"This is already almost too much for me. I can't do this. I actually never do things like this."

"That's fine. We're in it together."

"But I bet you do this all the time!"

"No, I don't. … You are special. I really love your energy. … There aren't many women out there who can completely enjoy the moment and are confident enough to go for what they want."

"But…, but you had left with my friend before you talked to me!"

I knew she would bring this up eventually. Since I had no idea what to say I made out with her again, which got her mind off this horrible thought. She did not want to enter the men's room with me, but maybe I could get her into the staircase and finish the job there? "What we are doing will be our little secret, OK?", I whispered in her ear. She stared into my eyes and nodded with an eager, "Yes!"

The stair case, however, was cordoned off. Not that I cared. We slipped in and ran up the first flight, hurried around the corner — and then the alarm went off. Fuck! We ran down again. I exploited this sudden burst of excitement by pressing her against the wall, making out some more, then switching positions. Now I was leaning against the wall. I pulled my cock out again and she immediately got to work. She was really amazing at it. Not many girls know how to give a decent handjob. We were staring into each other's eyes. "Come on, go a little bit faster!", I said.

Devil smiled and complied, while getting hornier and hornier herself as she whacked me off. She tremendously enjoyed this. Some heated minutes followed. I blew a load, which put a beautiful expression of lust and joy on her face. Being a gentleman I thanked her for it and kissed her again. I hugged her and asked her whether she had liked it. She kept looking into my eyes without saying a word. Then she smiled and wiped the cum on her index finger off my cheek, which made me laugh. We hugged, cuddled and made out some more. She wanted to rejoin her friends. I thought I would lose her if I let her go right now, so I decided to talk to her for a while about how rare it was for people to express their passions and follow their desires. In turn she mentioned that she had recently been to a fetish night, which she greatly enjoyed. Incidentally it was the very same

Torture Garden event I had been too as well.

I sensed that there was more fun to be had with DEVIL, but it seemed to be a good idea to rejoin her friends for a while. However, I had to clean up the mess on my T-shirt first and told her to wait for a moment. When I came back from the men's toilet some random dude was trying to chat her up. I pressed her against the wall and passionately made out with her again, before taking her back to her friends. The other guy did not even finish his sentence.

We danced for maybe fifteen or twenty minutes, but I was not really in the mood to dance. I was in the mood to return the favour. DEVIL apparently wanted more, so I dragged her off again. This time I found us a sofa in a more secluded area. Still, it was quite out in the open and people were passing by constantly. We sat down in the corner. She was sitting in my lap, leaning her back against the wall. In this position she could relax fairly well. After some light conversation and heavy making out I stuck my pinky up her cooch. I had been rubbing her pussy throughout the conversation, so this was no big deal for her anyway.

"I would love to suck on your marvellous breasts," I said. DEVIL smiled and invitingly pulled one of her straps down. I did the rest. They were the most amazing breasts I had ever seen. They were just perfect. I did not care that I could feel (small) implants. My pinky was still in her. She moved her pelvis rhythmically, so I switched fingers and added more thrust. Both her arms were wrapped around me and she was getting really into it. Her back arched first slowly, then heavily. She whispered in my ear, "This feels so good. … Aaah…. Oohhh…. Yeah, just like that! … Aaaah…. Oooohhh…. Aaaahhh…. Don't stop!"

After a few minutes her pussy contracted rhythmically. She pressed her fingernails into my back, and hard! This made me add more force to the thrusting movements of my arm. It was not easy to hide what we were doing. DEVIL did not hold back anything and screamed, "Ah.... Aah.... Aaah.... Aaaah.... AAAaahh.... AAAAAHH!" It was loud enough for people in a certain radius to hear. I felt like the man! After about fifteen seconds of her climaxing, heavily moaning and screaming loudly, people inevitably took notice. KOKO was already quite empty, but there were still enough people around. A random girl shrieked, "What is...? Oh my God! ... OH MY GOD!! LOOK!!" This alarmed all her friends and a chorus of five or six female voices erupted, shrieking, "AAAAARGH!!!"

Some other guy dared to come close and take a picture of me finger-banging DEVIL. I would have preferred getting up and smack this asshole one. However, I was more concerned about my girl's well-being, so I pulled my fingers out, covered her eyes with my hand and made out with her. I have been in potentially embarrassing situations before (well, not embarrassing for me), and it seemed best to not acknowledge the outside world or any kind of interference at all. I did exactly this and tongued her down hard. As I repositioned her so that she was more comfortable, one of my hands was free, which I used to give the bystanders the V sign, the insulting one, not the one denoting a victory. They finally buggered off. DEVIL seemed surprisingly unfazed by the whole scene. Amidst kisses she repeatedly thanked me for the orgasm. "Thank you, oh, thank you!", she said. It may sound incomprehensible to some, but I truly enjoyed this moment of public intimacy with her. It was more than exhibitionism, lust, and passion.

After a good ten minutes of making out things seemed safe

again. I even suspected that she got turned on heavily by the idea of having an orgasm in public, so the whole incident was probably much less of a big deal to her than I initially thought. Yet, I rather err on the safe side. We gazed into each other's eyes once again.

"Do you have a girlfriend?", she asked out of nowhere.

This is apparently what you get when you manage to get girls off.

"No, I don't. Do you want to apply?"

She laughed.

"I'd rather not. I just want to enjoy the moment with you."

"I could make you enjoy many more such moments."

She asked me the usual questions and said she would rather make this a one-time event. However, when I told her I was about to leave the U.K. she opened up some more. Knowing that I wouldn't be around for much longer, she seemed to consider the possibilities of meeting up again.

We were not quite done yet. After some more caressing and cuddling she was rubbing my crotch again. I moved her around on my lap, so that she was facing me with her legs spread. She unzipped my pants and eagerly whacked my cock moments later. I got a big erection. My cock was less than an inch away from her dripping wet pussy. Due to the way she was moving her body it already looked as if we were fucking. We might as well just do it "for real" I thought and announced that I had a condom. Devil uttered an undecided, "Um...." She said she did not want to and I made the mistake of listening to it. I slapped myself mentally. If there is one thing that won't get you any action at all, it is talking too much. I should just have pulled the condom out, slapped it on, and slid my cock in.

I am not quite sure, but I think the tip of my cock came in contact with her wet pussy at some point. At the very least, some of her juices were dripping down on it. I just get too carried away by passion at times. Heck, I probably would have fucked her without protection because we were both turned on so much. It is hard to keep a clear head in such heated moments.

Devil proceeded to give me a handjob, but I did not feel like blowing another load. I lifted her off my lap and sat her down right next to me. She was cuddling up to me and we were gently caressing each other. I also gave her a scalp massage and then a head massage, which she greatly enjoyed. She completely relaxed and slowed down her breathing. It was beautiful to watch and it was a nice way to end our encounter.

One shot, one kill

The previous day I had met two Swedish girls at Punk. They were actually the only ones there that were completely into me. We agreed to go out the next day and I had every intention of keeping my promise. At the very least I would have had some cool company and in the best case I would have ended up fucking the one that couldn't keep her hands off me. Even her friend encouraged her to hook up with me.

I told those girls to be at On The Rocks at around 11.30 p.m., while I planned to show up at 1 a.m. With some booze in their system I would have to do less work. Also, this was a polysexual, i.e. gay and lesbian night, so there was not much competition to be feared as I was one of the very few straight guys they let in anyway. At around midnight I was in the Shoreditch area.

First I went to the Hoxton Pony, a bar I read about online. I probably had been to every at least semi-popular venue in central London and it was getting increasingly difficult to find something new. The place looked all right from the outside, but the patrons inside did not. "Windowlicker" by Aphex Twin was playing, which was a pleasant surprise. The fat slobs trying to dance to it put me off, though. After two minutes I was out on the streets again. Traffik across the street was hardly any better.

After less than five minutes I wished the bouncer a good night. Electricity Showrooms was quite good, though.

Chocolate was the first interesting girl I saw. For a moment I considered approaching her straight away, but I decided to go downstairs to check out the dance floor first. I spotted a tall woman with a slim waist and huge knockers. Too bad her legs weren't that skinny. As I was about to go after her, Chocolate showed up. She was dancing with a female friend of hers and glancing over. I played it cool and kept dancing. She looked over to me again, which prompted me to take her hand and pull her in. We danced for a while, then she asked me to dance with her friend Plain. I have messed up a lot of similar situations because I mistook such requests as blow offs along the lines of, "I don't want to dance with you, but you can dance with my less attractive friend if you like." Instead, it seems to translate to, "I like you, and I want my friend to like you, too." Plain was not particularly good-looking, but I was fine with spinning her around a little bit. Chocolate was delighted and asked me the usual questions.

Then she tried to make me jealous by dancing with some other guy. I knew she was not serious about it, so I pulled her in again. Minutes later she said she wanted to get a drink with her friend. I replied that I would join them, but as she walked off she let go of my hand. I did not really care and continued dancing. Chocolate came back, looking for me. She wanted to go upstairs to the bar with Plain and I tagged along. I should have accepted her offer to buy me a drink. Telling her that tap water would be fine was probably a bit of an insult.

We all sat down. I kept my hands on Chocolate, but hidden from her friend. Plain had good manners and excused herself to smoke a cigarette. This allowed me to have some time alone with my girl. It must have been a really long cigarette because she was gone for easily ten minutes. We had some commonalities. Lucky me, she also spoke German because of an ex-boyfriend. CHOCOLATE gave me hints regarding her friend. She mentioned topics I should avoid and ones her friend might be interested in talking about. It's great when girls really want to hook up with you. PLAIN returned and CHOCOLATE said that we might go back to her place later on to listen to some music from the eighties.

Electricity Showrooms was about to close and those two girls wanted to go somewhere else to continue partying. They had been to the nearby club 333 Mother earlier and wanted me to join them. I didn't feel like shelling out £5, though. CHOCOLATE tried to argue with the guy at the door to get me in for free. In the meantime I told her friend that maybe it was not such a good idea to go to a club and that we probably would find it more enjoyable to go to a bar instead. CHOCOLATE came back. I immediately dragged her off, telling her about that great bar "just around the corner." Her friend chimed in that it was a really great place. I had treated PLAIN with respect and it paid off. Unfortunately Catch was about to close. CHOCOLATE now had to pee, so we went to another bar called The Spread Eagle. By that time she was already rather horny and touching me all over.

CHOCOLATE said she wanted to go back to her place. She then turned to me to say that I could go home if I wanted. I ignored this statement and said we should just get back to her place. On the way to her flat she wanted to buy something to eat. Once again she offered to buy me something and, again, I did not take her up on the offer. As I later found out, she was a medical professional and owned a really nice flat. She wanted to throw some money at me and I should have let her. Not that it mattered in any way in the end.

While she was waiting to get her kebab I talked to Plain outside. Having lived in Berlin seemed to really impress Londoners. Anyway, she also hinted at some things I should not bring up in conversation. When I randomly joked about how stuck-up the French are she dropped that French was Chocolate's first language. I could have run into serious trouble, but with the support of two girls who wanted me to get laid there wasn't much that could go wrong.

We missed the bus. Chocolate hailed a cab and we all hopped in. I was quite curious about the status of Plain. These two girls were not living together. Yet, she was about to come home with us. Would she have been more attractive I might have tried to push for a threesome, but, alas, she was not. The problem of how to get rid of her solved itself. In the flat we sat down in the living room and listened to some music. Chocolate pretty much excluded her friend from the conversation. First she asked me whether it was okay if *we* lit some candles. I had no objections. After that was done she suggested to burn some incenses. The atmosphere was already getting seductive. Her friend got the hint, made an excuse and said she wanted to leave. For some strange reason, however, Chocolate insisted that she slept in her other room.

At long last we were alone. We danced for a while in the living room, while running our hands up and down each other's bodies. Chocolate seemed to have some minor issues with kissing. She was not overly comfortable with it. However, when we were sitting on the sofa later on she was perfectly fine with me rubbing her pussy, which was more conducive to seduction anyway. Then I ran into a serious problem. It was around 3 a.m.

and she was apparently not used to staying up late. She slowly passed out. This was too bad because I already had her moaning. I should have wasted less time.

I was a bit confused and decided to text my buddy Terry. He found the situation hilarious and we joked around via SMS.

"I'm at a chick's house, and she just passed out. WTF?", I wrote.

"Touch her boobs!", he replied. Then he added:

"Good job getting her back to her house. That's basically almost as good as sex."

"Yeah, right! She's fucking hot and I wanna do her. I think I'll just wait a couple of hours. This sucks because I've got work to do."

It turned out that Chocolate was only somewhat asleep. I asked her whether I should take her to bed, to which she replied with a whispered, "Yes, please do so." I picked her up and carried her to the other room, where I laid her down on the bed. Then I asked her whether I should undress her to be more comfortable. I unbuttoned her pants, but as I wanted to pull them down she reflexively stopped me. I was a bit tired as well, so I just laid down next to her. Terry sent me another text message.

"Give her some water and something to eat if you can find it. It'll sober her up."

"She's passed out. Let's just hope she doesn't freak out in the morning."

Terry apparently got a real kick out of the situation. He fired off four messages in short succession.

"Ha! She will love you. Take care of her. Give her lots of water."

"And I reiterate. Touch her boobs."

"Just kidding. That's illegal."

"No boob!"

It was my turn again.

"Yeah. I'll just put my cock into her hand and let her wake up like this."

A few hours later Chocolate woke up and immediately cuddled up to me. I had decided not to sleep in my clothes and was only in underpants. Normally I sleep naked, but I found it a bit risky given the circumstances. She was rubbing her legs against mine and touching my chest. The first thing she said was that she had not intended that I stayed the night. I told her I could go home if she wanted me to, using my softest voice and gently touching her with my fingertips. She smiled at me and said she would like to wear something more comfortable. After a couple of minutes she came back in a nice nightgown that barely covered her ass. Her legs were really amazing. She jumped back into bed and cuddled up to me. I got hard. Of course Chocolate did not want to have sex because she did not knew me well enough, but less than ten seconds later she was already playing with my cock.

Chocolate became the woman I spent most time with for the remainder of my stay in London. She treated me like a king and spent quite a bit of money on me. All I gave her in return were shattering orgasms. I also taught her how to give proper blowjobs. Other men should be thankful for that.

The joy of juggling

Random dates

I had not been going out for a while because I was busy fucking CHOCOLATE. After a couple of weeks I got a bit bored of her, however, and decided to try something new for a change: I set up a couple of dates. I usually did not follow up on the telephone numbers I occasionally collected because I found it too burdensome to meet up with people in London.

Originally I had set up two dates, one with PINK at 8 p.m. and the other with ITALIAN at 10 p.m. PINK did not show up. I called her but only got her voice mail, so I texted her that I would be somewhere close to the meeting point and that she could drop by when she is in the area. I walked over to Hoxton Square to read a book. At around 9 p.m. I received a frantic text message from her, saying that she had to work overtime, that her phone got busted and that she was "feeling like a bitch."

ITALIAN showed up, though. I had met her some weeks ago at a bar but I had almost forgotten about her. One morning I found myself whacking off to mental images of her. Thus I texted her, "Sorry for not staying in touch. I have been really busy lately.

Wanna hang out next week?" It did the trick. I may sound like a complete asshole, but I honestly could not remember her face anymore, only her ass and legs. When a girl walked up to me, smiling and overly happy to see me, it took me more than a split-second to realise that this must be her. I had to put away the book I was reading anyway, so there was nothing odd about my slightly delayed response.

After an intense hug we trotted down to T Bar, a small electro venue. On the way she was already all over me and touching me all the time. At the bar she pulled out her company credit card and ordered what struck me as relatively expensive red whine. I couldn't remember ever having paid £5 or £6 for a small glass, but I didn't have to pay for it so I didn't mind. Her company had to foot the bill and I hope they didn't mind either. An expense account seems to be a cool thing to have. Even though I don't drink and I am always sober when going out, the occasional glass of red whine is fine with me. It is supposed to be healthy, I like the taste, and I don't really feel any effect.

Our conversation went quite well. We couldn't keep our hands off each other. I was not quite sure whether it was a good idea to let her talk so much, but when a girl talks about her subconsciousness I always let her babble on. In short, she was cuddling up to me while we were chatting and drinking. Then she described one of her roommates to me and dropped that I would meet her. Apparently she already saw herself lying in bed with me.

We went outside for a while. She smoked a cigarette and I enjoyed the fresh air. Back inside I dragged her over to the dance floor and worked my magic. What I liked most about ITALIAN was that she truly loved getting dominated. She pushed me away, but every time I pulled her in forcefully she rewarded me by either grinding her ass hard against my cock, sucking on my neck or grabbing my ass. Apparently she got off on the attention. She remarked, "Everyone is watching us." I doubted this because the place was quite empty and most of the patrons had a disinterested look on their faces.

One thing put me off, though: she didn't let me kiss her on the lips. On the other hand, she was fine with me sucking her neck as long as I did not leave a hickey. In response to her bizarre statement that she only wanted us to be "dance buddies" I grabbed one of her belt loops, pulled her in forcefully, grabbed her hair, yanked her head back and licked her neck. She said she had to get to know me better before doing more, i.e. kissing and everything beyond.

I felt I had not had enough time to work on her and unfortunately she had to leave at midnight. Expense accounts apparently only come with jobs. For the record, she worked fourteen hours a day and I worked zero. We made plans to meet up next week and she promised to "do more" then. She sounded like a lot of work and her perv factor was minuscule. It did not bother me much that we never met again.

Two crushes in one night

About one minute later I was already looking around for other prospects. Blue was the first attractive girl to enter my field of vision. I am positive that she had seen me with Italian, which is a relevant piece of information for later. She wore a blue top, in case you find her name odd. This girl was from Spain and easily an 8 on the looks scale. Apparently she was part of a larger group, but to me it was not quite clear who was part of it and who wasn't. One guy definitely was. He told me he had five apartments in five cities: London, New York City, Berlin, Milan and somewhere else, and worked as a designer. Then he said he was only twenty years old. I did not really know what to make of it. He was dressed in a really cool way, so there could at least have been some truth to it, read: obnoxious rich kid. Because he was very cooperative there was absolutely no point in getting inquisitive or confrontational. Heck, if I told people that I am used to getting handjobs from random girls on the dance floor within minutes they probably would not believe me either.

After chatting with the guy he introduced me to his two female friends. Of course I could have approached BLUE directly in the first place, but by getting introduced by her friend I started off in a much better position. I shook the hand of the other girl in the group before I turned to BLUE. A hand shake easily transitions into a spin, so I did that. She asked me whether I knew her friend and afterwards she fired off the usual questions. Because she was already touching me, I pulled her in, made out with her, and tried to drag her off to a sofa. At first she was strangely reluctant, but it emerged that she only wanted to tell her friends that she was joining me. Furthermore, she did not want to leave her handbag behind.

I let her sit on my lap and we explored each other's bodies. The whole interaction was fairly sexual. However, by breaking the make outs and offering pieces of information about myself I did not run the risk of being perceived as yet another "tacky club make out guy." It was so easy to connect with her that it should have scared me. Is it really that simple? Whenever she said something I transitioned with "that's great/amazing/whatever, because I did/know/have been...." She did the same. After less than fifteen minutes we had established a relatively bizarre "soul mate vibe." BLUE was enormously attracted to me. I had no choice but to like her as well.

BLUE basically told me she would love to fuck me. No, she did not use these very words. When I commented that it was too bad that she had to take care of her friends and couldn't leave them behind she said, "I know. It's bad timing, but I'd really love to." She had friends staying in her room which she could not or did not want to leave on her own. Therefore we agreed to hook up the following Saturday. I told her where I lived and that we could meet up close by and go back to mine after walking around for a bit. She was staring into my eyes the whole time. Actually, it was difficult to talk to her because she incessantly wanted to kiss me. It was really cute.

After about an hour her friends wanted to leave and BLUE left with them. I decided to stay at T Bar because the music had picked up. Thirty minutes later it was nonetheless time to go somewhere else. At 1.00 a.m. it was definitely too early to call it a night.

I knew about a semi-decent club night nearby, because I had been there some weeks ago. However, I had problems finding it. I asked a girl on the street for the way, but she walked past without acknowledging my presence. I immediately turned to the next guy and asked him. He was clueless. For whatever reason, the girl now stormed back to me. Maybe she had taken a closer look at me. She excitedly told me that the club night I wanted to go to was only once a month, and volunteered some random information about herself and this area. I quizzed her for a bit, but I walked off after a while because I was not especially interested.

Mother Bar was close by. It is a somewhat eccentric bar with a small dance floor. On Thursday it attracted a rather eclectic crowd, meaning there was a fair chance of bumping into hot tourists. In my experience it was always a bit of a gamble, though, but I could not think of anywhere else to go. To my great disappointment the crowd was mostly obnoxiously drunk and noisy. As I was about to turn around and leave I spotted Blue again. I was surprised because she had told me she had to get up for work at 5 a.m. I don't like girls that bullshit me, but she explained that she had accidentally run into one of her best friends. Thus she had to continue partying. She was very happy to see me and was very sweet. There was lots of touching, kissing, and a couple of make outs thrown in between. I joined her friends for a while and they all loved me.

Someone else loved me as well, an insanely attractive Italian girl. (I seem to have a thing for Italians.) Her black dress nicely accentuated her figure and tight body. I'll call her Tight. She was easily a 9 in my book. With sparkling eyes and a huge smile she came up to me and asked me whether I had been to Madame Jojo's earlier this week. I had, but I could not remember having seen her. She stared at me and bit her lip.

Apparently the Pick-up God in the heavens decided to present me with another gift. Thanks a bunch, buddy! For a moment I was unsure what to do. In my head, Cosy's voice told me to jump ship. (Of course I did.) I was fully aware that this would severely piss off Blue, but I felt immensely attracted to Tight. I had no other choice. Besides, Blue has had a fair shot at getting with me. Instead of losing another hour of sleep to party with one of her friends she could as well have blown me in an alley.

Within ten seconds I was making out with Tight. People seem to notice when you make out with the hottest girl in the venue in the middle of the dance floor. Blue's friends took notice, and

Blue did as well. She looked severely disappointed. However, as I had mentioned before, I am pretty sure she had witnessed Italian sucking on my neck earlier that night. She should thus have come to the conclusion that I was a bit of a slut. To make it perfectly clear: I would have regretted not going after Tight and I am glad I did. You can't have every girl.

Blue's designer friend put his hand on my shoulder and told me in an aggressive tone of voice, "You've fucked it up, dude. You've fucked it up! … She would have fucked you, and she would have fucked you good." I shrugged it off. My arrogant former self would have said one of two things. Either I would have asked him rhetorically what he thought I intended to do with Tight, with a smug grin on my face, or I would have dropped that I was seeing another girl regularly anyway. I probably would have said both. In this case I could only say that I was sorry. For a moment I felt bad about myself. Because I really had connected with Blue I realised that I must have hurt her. I may sound like a real dick, but having Tight's hands running over my body while she was sucking out my fillings helped me getting over these momentarily self-doubts quickly.

Some minutes later I was sitting on a sofa with Tight in my lap. We connected on almost the same topics as I had before with Blue. Tight was staying with friends but was on vacation in London for four more weeks. We agreed to go to Tate Modern together because of our shared interest in contemporary art. I suggested Saturday instead of Sunday or Monday to see how interested she was. The idea excited her. To spice up our conversation I told her things like, "You turn me on so much," and, "We shouldn't do this. … This is way too much way too soon, but it is too hard to resist you." I thought it was a bit corny, but those statements had quite an effect on her. They became mainstays of my game afterwards.

While rubbing my chest Tight told me that men should not wear glittery T-shirts. I explained to her why I like gay culture so much and added that I love to look gay, to which she of course had to ask me whether I was. I did not say anything and looked into her eyes for a few seconds before kissing her again. She also rhetorically asked whether she should really get with a guy like me and dropped that she would have to find out whether I was a good boy or a bad boy first, because she only trusted good boys. I am of course more of a bad boy, so I grabbed her hair, pulled her head down and licked her neck before kissing her again. I said that she liked bad boys better anyway and she agreed with a huge smile. This girl was good at playing the game.

One of her female friends dropped by and Tight introduced me to her. I complimented the guy she was with on his choice of colours. He had matched an interesting red and brown tone, which looked interesting. Because he had no real sense of fashion he ate up my words. It was a genuine compliment, nonetheless. Obviously, he loved me as well after that. I also found it interesting that when I parted from Tight another girl came up to say goodbye, followed by yet another one of her friends. I guess this was all due to the positive aura I had created and spread.

On my way home I suffered through the repercussions of the night. I really did like both girls and felt bad for disappointing Blue. Maybe I had developed two crushes in about two hours. It felt good to truly connect with a girl and to realise that she liked me for more than my looks. Of course I had forgotten about Blue within seconds of making out with Tight, so I had no reason to complain about anything. But on the other hand I felt sad for a moment when I saw the disappointment in Blue's eyes. It was as if I had broken her heart, if only just a little bit.

Accepting the gift

Originally I intended to meet up with Tight on Saturday. However, I had spent Friday evening with Chocolate and left her house next day at around 4 p.m. Because there are only so many times a day you want to fuck I texted Tight that I could not meet her but that I would be free on Sunday. She already had plans for that day, so we agreed to meet Monday noon in front of Tate Modern. I had picked this place because it was in walking distance to my flat.

She was late. At 12.15 p.m. I gave her a call and it turned out she was waiting at the other entrance. We hugged and she kissed me on the cheeks. This was a bit cold compared to the amount of affection I had received on Thursday night. Then again, it was Monday noon, so a tongue-down in broad public would probably have been out of the question anyway. We spent some time in the exhibition. A lot of young girls eyeballed me excessively. Apparently they did not get to see many rockstars — or pretenders like me. The highlight was a group of little girls, ranging from maybe twelve to fourteen, who followed me around for a while, openly staring at me and giggling. When I turned around to face them they blushed and turned their little heads, but when I walked over to Tight and took her hand they quickly buggered off. Poor little things! After the first floor Tight still showed some reserve. But on the escalator to the second floor I pulled her in to kiss her on the lips. She immediately shoved her tongue down my throat, which came as a bit of a surprise.

We spent around two hours in the building, held hands occasionally and made out a couple of times. We did not talk that much. Then again, I can communicate all the right things nonverbally. Eventually we had seen everything there was to see. TIGHT seemed sufficiently horny and all I had to do now was to get her back to my place.

In front of Tate Modern we sat down on a bench. I pulled her down on my lap and we made out for a while. I finally got the same level of attention as on Thursday at 2 a.m. Unfortunately the weather was not that great. I mentioned that I would love to take her to St James' Park and cuddle with her. She excitedly interrupted me by asking whether I wanted to go there with her right now. Cuddling in the cold grass did not sound overly enticing to me, though, so this was not really an option. Besides, it would not have helped me much in terms of seduction. I asked her whether she was hungry because I wanted to cook some fish and said that she would be welcome to join me. She gladly accepted my invitation.

Probably I was playing the whole date way too safe. I think I could have taken her back to my place right away and skipped the art exhibition, dinner and the cathedral we visited. Yes, there was a cathedral on the way: Southwark Cathedral. Afterwards we went to a nearby supermarket and bought some food. TIGHT was already quite submissive. She knew what was about to go down. I asked her what she liked but she could not come up with suggestions. Therefore I picked some things, asked whether she liked them and made my way to the checkout. I paid for it, but it was no big deal because the total cost of the food only amounted to around £4. I had picked fish and leaf spinach, which are both light and healthy, because I did not want to stuff her.

Back at my place things went smoothly. We went into my room, dropped off some stuff, then went into the kitchen and prepared the meal. I let her assist me in cooking. Later on I fed her. I really liked the whole atmosphere. After cleaning the dishes I took her back to my room. I sat down on the bed and pulled her in to make out with her for a few moments. Then I got up to brush my teeth, just in case. She got the hint and asked me whether she could use the bathroom as well. I had some mouthwash, which she used. (I was unaware that brushing your teeth before oral sex increases the risk of transmitting STDs.)

Moments later we picked up where we had left off. Things got hot and heavy in no time. After five minutes of devouring each other, our clothes were mostly off already. When I went for her panties I got token resistance. After a few more minutes of heavily making out they finally went off. My fingers went in.

In all honesty there were quite a few issues. The first one was that she was about to get on the rag. I made her moan with my mighty middle and index fingers, but when I pulled them out there was quite a bit of blood on them. I did not mind at all, but she made countless excuses. After some cuddling and kissing this problem was dealt with and she proceeded to give me the best blowjob of the year so far, including deep-throating. I was impressed. So far I had no problems, but then I rolled on a condom. My performance was quite substandard. The loose grip of her pussy did not help matters either. I could not keep it up for long. For what it's worth, though, I think she was amazing in the sack.

Yet, it was disappointing that neither of us got off. In the end, a very pleasurable seventy minutes — or a good four hours, depending on how you see it — were marred. After extensive foreplay and one attempt at actual sex she rolled off. I only got to the brink of busting a nut, and she also only got close to an orgasm. It was building up in her body, but it eventually dissipated. I felt bad about myself afterwards. After some minutes of lying right next to each other, she said that she should probably go. We dressed and I took her to the tube station.

Frankly speaking, TIGHT was the hottest girl I have had sex with up to that point. Unfortunately I was too much in my head, always asking myself whether I did it right and whether she liked what I was doing. She was also very eager to please me. Maybe we had similar issues. My self-doubts even affected my voice, which became a bit brittle. At the tube station we kissed passionately and with lots of tongue. I dropped that we should go out sometime. She agreed but, alas, we never met again.

The pessimistic turn of my description of this encounter puzzled me for quite a while. In hindsight, I can only shake my head that it took me several days before I was able to appreciate that I had an Italian girl of exceptional beauty in my bed. I fooled around with her extensively and received an amazing blowjob. Furthermore, her pussy felt really great. Objectively speaking there was no real reason to complain about anything.

My first three-way make out and other antics

Being chronically short of money, I had to move to a pretty bad neighbourhood recently. On my way to the tube station two idiots called me a fag and shouted some other random expletives at me. They would not have dared to challenge me on their own. I ignored them and walked past. This is a good example for the kind of shit I semi-regularly have to deal with. However, my access to pussy certainly helps putting such minor annoyances into perspective.

The night was off to a great start: the bouncer at Madame Jojo's let me in for free, asking me where I had been! In a way, this was also bad news because I had prepared a handful of small change for paying cover charge. Inside I bumped into TERRY. We had a bit of a fallout recently and hadn't been speaking for a couple of weeks. He told me to "go fuck yourself" or something along these lines. Two weeks later we were best friends again, though.

On the almost empty dance floor a group of four very excited girls caught my attention, and attention was all those slutty-looking girls wanted. I walked up to them, grabbed the hand of Easy, who looked like the most eager girl of them all and dragged her away from her friends. She excitedly screamed, "Wooo! WOOOO!!" I found it fairly annoying, to be honest. Moments later we were dancing close and one of her friends joined in. Now both were humping my legs. Easy's friend eventually buggered off. After some intense grinding and mutual ass grabbing we made out. I decided to leave it at that. Those girls seemed to be too much in party mode and I was not really in the mood for my usual perversions. I only wanted to dance. Easy asked me whether she could climb on my shoulders. I let her and felt like an idiot with her waving her hands and incessantly screaming, "WOOO!! WOOOO!!!" After a few moments I let her down again. She wandered off.

I talked to some girls in the bar area for about half an hour, and when I went back to the dance floor I saw that Easy and her friends had taken off their tops in the meantime. They were dancing in their bras and chanting, "Single! Single!", while downing shots. This sounded like quite a mating call to me, so I swooped in and hip-bumped one of those girls. Moments later Easy and another girl had their hands all over me and under my T-shirt. They apparently wanted to undress me and tore on my clothes. I was afraid they would ruin something, so I told them to calm down and ordered Easy to take my T-shirt off slowly. Both were now running their hands over my naked upper body. Easy cooed and said to her friend, "Oh, look at his chest!", while rubbing it. The whole scene caused quite a stir. I was half-naked, the two girls in my arms were dancing suggestively and only wore a bra, miniskirt and high-heels. The other two girls of Easy's group were cheering us on. After a few moments all eyes were on us, including the eyes of the bouncer that had let me in for free. With a stern voice he told me to put my T-shirt back on.

After this intermezzo the two girls rubbed their bodies against me. They exchanged glances. Two seconds later I found myself in my first three-way make out. This sounds much cooler than it was as it was way too sloppy for my taste. I left in the middle of it because of the most amazing girl I had seen in a long time. She was a quarter Chinese and had, as she later put it, a "Western" and well proportioned body but the typical Asian black silk hair as well as the typical white complexion. I think I developed an insta-crush on her.

We danced for a while and, because she was so small, slim and petite, I twirled her around and dipped her repeatedly, which she loved. This also caused a major spectacle. Quickly a circle of about a dozen people formed. They were hollering and clapping. I took this as an excuse to get her outside "to have some privacy." Too bad she was only a tourist. She was a bit cold and the vibe was just not there, but she complimented me on my skills on the dance floor. I took her number and got a peck on my lips. I could hardly understand her accent anyway.

Back inside I literally bumped into Boobs. She was more of the voluptuous kind: enormous juggs, but certainly a pound or two too much. Well, her boobs were great. I pulled her in and immediately went for the kiss. She turned her head away and asked me whether I was gay. I put my hand on her neck and stared into her eyes. Then we kissed. According to her I was "too good a kisser to be straight." This girl was about a 7 lookswise, even though her boobs were a 9. Yet, I did not feel like continuing with her and let her go.

On the dance floor I saw a fairly cool guy. He was very aggressive and generally tried to kiss the girls within seconds. There was one he seemingly wanted to approach. I found her attractive as well, so I swept right in. He walked up to me afterwards and jokingly complained about my rude behaviour. I liked him and decided to team up with him. When I asked him whether he was a "player" he smiled and said he did not quite understand what that term meant. But then he complained that there were no attractive girls in the club anymore. He was wrong, though, because two hot girls were dancing to the right of us. I pushed one of them into his arms and focused on the other myself. He could not handle the situation. Apparently I had overestimated him.

My longtime favourite Big Hair was also around. However, these days she refused to make out with me. Apparently I was too much of a slut for her. I hit on one of her friends without knowing. She asked me whether I was Aaron and introduced herself. For some reason this immediately brought her from "flirty mode" to "friendly conversation mode." Maybe she found it weird to flirt with friends of her friends.

Despite greatly enjoying my time at Madame Jojo's I was craving for an edgier experience. Hence, I took a short walk to my favourite gay watering hole Ghetto, which was further up the street. To my surprise there were four girls with fake boobs in the club. Usually there are not many of those around, at least not of the ridiculously large kind.

The first two just had great and extremely well proportioned bodies. One of them was busy. Luckily it was the hotter one who was unoccupied. I high-fived her and wanted to pull her in. Two of her friends interrupted us, apparently a gay guy and a lesbian. Both hustled me to kiss them on the cheek. After exchanging the usual niceties they walked off. The girl said that she was only into women, but she said it in a way that made me lose my erection. Her voice was deeper than most men's. Was this a post-op transvestite? She wore extremely tight pants, so I found it unlikely that there was a dick hiding somewhere in those. I did not want to find out, though. Indeed, there was an uncanny subtle masculinity to her face and her legs looked a bit too good anyway. On a side note, did you know that most if not all leg models are male? That's right, the beautiful legs they advertise tights with, in the pictures you may have whacked off to in your early teens, are more often than not the shaved legs of a man.

I spotted a group of three, consisting of a gay guy, an obvious lesbian and REDHEAD. I pulled REDHEAD in and she asked me what I wanted. I told her I only wanted to dance. Heck, considering her level of compliance I should have told her I wanted to bang her in a dark alley. She was voluptuous and a masterful cocktease. The most I got was her fingers scratching my pubic area. No, she did not touch my cock, but she repeatedly kissed my neck. However, she taught me something new by lifting up my T-shirt and her top and pressing the naked skin of our upper bodies tightly against each other.

Two other girls looked completely out of place. My best bet was that they were gold diggers. The first one was absurdly tanned, had fake blonde hair and wore pink lipstick. She was already occupied with a guy who played "buy drinks and get nothing later." I tried to save her from him by taking her hand and spinning her around, but she told me she was busy with "someone" already. For a moment I thought about pushing the interaction further, but looking at her up-close almost made me want to puke. She should have quit tanning years ago.

Her friend looked like a comic figure. She was around 5'9" and her boobs were bigger than her head. I am not kidding. I danced with Comic Figure for a while and she ground her ass against my cock just fine. She was with a rather boring looking guy she seemed to be somewhat close to. For instance, she told me about some of their travels. Apparently she found me sufficiently interesting and did not at all mind that I was fondling her breasts while talking to her. I kept squeezing one of her boobs simply because I had to. Then I did some of my usual stuff like lifting her up, turning her around in the air and the like. She cooed that she could not believe how strong I was. Well, I am not pumped, but I am strong and I have barely any body fat, which makes for an impressive body. There was nothing to be gained from that interaction and I found Comic Figure to be a tad too infantile for my taste. Thus I went home, only to whack off to mental images of her.

I bumped into Comic Figure and her dude again some weeks later. It emerged that he played in a third-rate band. He even referred to himself as "rockstar." After he was done bragging he complained that I was hitting on his *wife*. By the way, his band has a rather lengthy and badly written article on Wikipedia. I haven't yet bothered to listen to any of their music, though.

Pulling a cokehead from a gay club

Learning experiences

I was supposed to meet up with Ganja. We wanted to go to a club night where friends of hers were DJing, but she flaked relatively late because she was feeling "really unwell." I didn't have other plans, so I decided on a whim to go to one of the biggest gay nights in London, which is hosted at Sin. Unfortunately there seemed to only be a fairly limited number of straight girls who go to gay nights. In a small club you might have a decent selection of those, but in large venues their absolute number could very well be the same. I had gotten hold of a flyer for free entry and decided to give it a shot anyway. It was worse than expected. There were barely any girls in the place and attractive ones where almost nowhere to be seen. This was probably due to the enormous size of this club. A small and edgy night has a completely different appeal. But Sin did not take many risks regarding the music.

Some girls are just chubby. You can poke your fingers into their flesh and they might not even notice it. In front of me was In-

DIAN. She was certainly not slim, but her body was very firm and so were her ass and tits. After a high five I turned her around so that she could grind her ass against my groin. I put her hand on my crotch and she happily rubbed it. Then I turned her around, heated her up some more by fondling her breasts and transitioned into grinding. This time I shoved her hand down my pants. Seconds later she was massaging my cock, which put her in a trance. Unfortunately I let go of her for a few seconds too long, which probably made her realise that she had just rubbed my junk. She stared at me incredulously and walked off with a perplexed smile on her face. I always feel great when random girls stroke my cock.

After this intermezzo I walked downstairs to the "love lounge," where they played cheesy R'n'B tracks. There was a group of four girls that looked completely out of place. This made them perfect targets. I pulled the hottest one out of this circle. "Hot" did not mean much in this context because these girls were ranging from 5 to 7 on the looks scale. The one I was busy with only had a nice rack. Her face was really not that great. While dancing she rattled off the usual questions. After I had deflected them she jokingly asked me whether I was aware that she was not a man. She wasn't that ugly, mind you. While sliding my lower lip over her neck I mumbled that I was not gay. This made her nervous, but I just laughed and told her that she didn't have to be afraid of anything since according to her I was gay anyway. This little role play went on for a while, but eventually I got bored of her and left.

Later on I spotted her again in a hallway. As she was walking past I grabbed her hand and pulled her in close. She immediately pressed her pelvis against mine. I didn't have any intention to progress with her. In such cases I say and do the most extreme things I can think of, just to see how far I can go. She teased me by asking why a straight guy would want to go to a gay club anyway. I cut her off and calmly told her that I could easily prove to her that I was straight. She gave me a curious look. I tried putting her hand on my crotch. She would not let me do it and giggled.

This girl was strangely fascinated by my boldness. I said I could prove it in another way and offered her to suck my cock in the toilets. Those were my very words. I held strong eye contact while describing how amazing it would be for her to run her tongue up and down my warm hard throbbing cock. She got visibly nervous and parroted back to me, "I don't want to run my tongue up and down your warm hard throbbing cock." It was pretty amusing. I said I was sure that she had just gotten completely wet. She denied, but when I put my hand under her skirt to feel her panties she playfully slapped it away. She giggled nervously and was amused. Not in the least was she offended. I pulled her in again.

Of course she had to lead the conversation somewhere else. Otherwise she would have gotten out of control. She mentioned her boyfriend. This was great because girls don't seem to bring this issue up a lot when dealing with me. They simply "forget" about it. I told her that she would have four or five children with her "nice boyfriend" and live happily ever after in the country, to which she replied that he was "indeed very rich and has a huge mansion in the countryside." Apparently this was exactly what she wanted. I am pretty sure she was bullshitting, though. I told her I did not want to ruin her relationship and let her go. At first I thought I might go back to her later, but then I bumped into a rather attractive blonde.

Luckily her gay friend's bed was empty

COKEHEAD was a petite blonde. I made eye contact with her and raised my hand for a high five. She didn't react to it. Thus I took her hand and pulled her in. At first she was a bit resistant, but I could tell that this was all just an act she put on. After less than one minute we were dancing close while our hands were running up and down each other's bodies. She told me she had a boyfriend. I asked her whether he was in the venue. This was probably a bad move, but because I had been on the brink of getting into a physical confrontation with not one but two pissed off boyfriends earlier that week I wanted to play it safe for a change. She said he wasn't. Consequently I said to her that she should enjoy the moment and not worry about anything else.

She asked where *my* boyfriend was. I told her I was straight and that I mostly go out on my own, which she both found remarkable. Her two gay friends soon joined us. Gay guys accept me quickly because they think I am one of them. After a while COKEHEAD wanted to get drinks with them. She seemed too interested to just leave, so I let her walk off after a passionate hug. A few minutes later she came back. She had lost her two gay friends in the meantime. Now we could dance alone for a while. I did my best to arouse her and indirectly stimulated her by massaging some pressure points on her lower back and ass. After some moments she asked me whether I wanted to join her group for the night.

Her situation was fairly complicated and I could only reconstruct it in hindsight. In the club I could make neither head or tail of it. This is how it was: she lived in Islington and so did the two gay friends she was with. Those two guys shared a flat but were not romantically involved with each other. That night COKEHEAD was staying at their place, even though she lived just up the road. It would have been unnecessary for her to stay over, but apparently they were very close friends. We could not get back to her place for a reason she did not want to reveal.

My guess was that she was living with her boyfriend but had a fight, so she preferred to stay with her two gay friends. The two gay guys shared a bed that night so that COKEHEAD could have the other one. This was already complicated enough, but it only went worse as the night progressed: one of the gay guys hooked up with another guy, which was good. Bad was that the other gay guy's ex-boyfriend of three years showed up at SIN. Three years in gayland are apparently the equivalent of a two-hundred year relationship of a straight couple, so this understandably dragged him down. I'll come back to this later.

I joined COKEHEAD's group and we went into another room. She had already taken quite a liking to me. However, even after some ass grabbing and crotch rubbing she was still reluctant to kiss me. She had a quick chat with her two gay friends. Then she turned back to me and immediately tongued me down. This was the turning point in our interaction. Later on she told me that when she saw me she thought I was "hot but also tripping on E because you seemed so blissful." After spending some time with me she realised that she liked me, so she had to check with her friends whether they also thought that I was hot. Girls and their insecurities! Their approval gave COKEHEAD the permission she needed. I shoved her hand down my pants and she excitedly played with my cock for a while. She then complained that I was naughty and I retorted that she was naughty, too. This made her protest, "But it's because you make me!"

Cokehead avoided being alone with me. She was probably, and rightly so, afraid she would lose control. However, her gay friends wanted her to hook up. The first occasion to get her alone was when she wanted to get another drink. While she was leaning against the bar to order I pressed my body against hers. Then I pulled my cock out, so that it was outside my pants but hidden under my T-shirt. I guided her hand down there. She did not touch it for long, though, but she gave me a couple of proper strokes behind her back. I pressed her harder against the bar, which made her say that I should not dry hump her. Nonetheless she moved her pelvis suggestively while I was rhythmically rubbing the shaft of my hard cock against her butt. She seemed delighted.

Cokehead repeatedly dropped that I was a *really* great kisser and that she *really* liked me and all that jazz. We rejoined her gay friends and she asked me whether I wanted to be with her tonight. I did notice the ambiguity. Since some women only seek the validation that comes from knowing that they could get a guy they fancied, I reacted as if I assumed she had meant to spend the rest of the night in the club with her.

We went outside where I watched her smoke a cigarette. Her gay friends stayed back and told her it would be all right because I would take good care of her. Eventually she revealed that she did not have a boyfriend anymore but broke up with him some weeks ago. Then she said that she was more the relationship kind of girl. Her two previous relationships both lasted about three years each. She got into the first at the age of sixteen. After a hiatus of two weeks she entered the second one, which was the one that had ended recently. Presumably she wanted to make the point that she was available, but only for something more serious. However, she also said, "We won't have sex tonight." When uttered by a woman this usually means the exact opposite.

She also added that I should not think she was a slut for making out with me that quickly. I told her that I like passionate girls and that there was nothing wrong with losing oneself in the moment. "But I did touch your cock!", she blurted out. I repeated that I like passionate girls that just go for what they want and mentioned that I considered it wrong to be judgemental about people who want to express themselves. More hugs and kisses ensued. COKEHEAD still refused to believe that I was sober and tried to tease me about it. I don't react to such bullshit. She then confessed that she had snorted some lines of coke already.

It was around 2.30 a.m. COKEHEAD said she wanted to leave at around 3 a.m., which was fine with me. The only thing left was collecting her friends. One of those guys had hooked up with another guy in the meantime, as I mentioned. COKEHEAD had a quick chat with him. I can only assume that she asked him whether it was okay if she shared her bed with me tonight, because the next thing she said was, "Do you want to stay with me tonight?" I agreed and because she insisted on it I also agreed not to have sex with her. Of course, this was utter nonsense.

Her other gay friend was quite heartbroken. COKEHEAD urged him to "just hook up with someone, anyone!" He did not seem to like her idea. Finally we left. On the way out, she asked me whether I really wanted to leave and that I could stay in the club if I wanted to. I ignored this question. We could only find an illegal taxi. I made the mistake of throwing in £10. The ride was £15 for the three of us and the guy promised to pay me back at home. However, I forgot about it when we were back at his place. On the ride Cokehead joked that she would be worth the ten pounds.

We were in the guy's rather impressive flat at around 3 a.m. Cokehead told me that his parents had paid the £500,000 for it in cash. We hung out in the living room for a while. In fact, we hung out for far too long there, probably an hour or so. The atmosphere was sexual nonetheless. She excitedly told her friend, "He just shoved my hand down his pants!" He did not care at all and nonchalantly asked whether I had a "big willie." (I think I do.) While we were sitting on the sofa, she was openly rubbing my crotch in front of her friend. She even went down on her knees once and rubbed my thighs as if she was about to pull down my pants and suck my cock. Of course she was only teasing me, but it got me rock hard. I almost had to laugh at her statement, "I said we won't have sex. But don't worry, because I give the best blowjobs."

While chilling in the living room and listening to music she suddenly asked the nasty question, "What's my name?" I had forgotten it and openly admitted it. In reply she asked me how I could forget my future daughter's name. Earlier at Sin I had told her that her name was among the few I considered for my first daughter, which was true. Luckily this made me remember it. At around 4 a.m. the guy went to bed. I stayed back with Cokehead and cuddled with her on the sofa. She seemed to like this a lot and suggested to have a "six-week summer romance." It was time to go to bed.

This girl was much less sexual and cool about it than I expected. Suddenly, she wanted to do everything right. I undressed her and let my hands run over her legs. She stopped me and giggled, saying that she did not expect to meet a straight guy at a gay club. Asking for her reason for bringing this up again she conceded that she had not shaved her legs. She hushed into the bathroom to shave them for me. I found this somewhat cute, but it ruined the vibe. Also, because blondes have thinner hair anyway, it would have been a complete non-issue.

After she came back I lied her down on the bed and kissed her. Her lips had an unpleasantly bitter taste. She licked them and nonchalantly told me that this was "just coke." I proceeded by stimulating her clit. It did turn her on, but she refused to let me get her off. She even claimed that she usually didn't orgasm at all. Considering that she got tense when an orgasm built up, this was obviously a serious issue. She would have cum easily had she allowed herself to relax. I even got the impression that she was unable to enjoy sex. It felt somewhat off with her. The blowjob she gave me was indeed very good, though.

We woke up at 11 a.m. and she refused to kiss me. She was quite reserved and said she usually was "not up for doing naughty things in the morning." Sobered up she did not at all seem to be sexually liberated. She blurted out that she did not really know me. I deflected this and jokingly asked her the usual questions. She still knew all the details. Then I said that it was apparently not that bad and that she knew a lot about me. We cuddled for a while. COKEHEAD reiterated that she really liked me and told me about two other guys that were interested in her. One was a needy douchebag: "He is 6'4", but he is bald, so you are better than him!" The other one she was on a date with the previous week. He did not have the balls to touch her. She openly said I fit her bill perfectly, but also that it was a shame that I would leave London in a couple of weeks. We eventually hugged and kissed some more and she grabbed my junk as her way of saying goodbye.

For the record, COKEHEAD held a degree from University College London, had a respectable job and seemingly had her life together. Unfortunately all she seemed to be interested in was a long-term relationship, which was probably part of the reason for her odd behaviour in the morning. She also openly told me that she wanted to have her first child at twenty-seven. If she had not met Mr. Right by then she would "just take the best available candidate." At thirty-two she wanted to repeat this process.

I think I could have met her again had I not told her that I was about to leave London. On the other hand, to a "stable" woman I hardly look like the kind of guy to have a relationship with and the idea of exclusivity was foreign to me anyway. I should not complain because I got an amazing blowjob out of it. It did set me back ten pounds, though.

Recruiting a masterful cocksucker

My plan for the night was to meet up with Devil. She was busy with flat hunting, so these plans fell through. I had to go out on my own and decided to go to *Club NME* at KOKO, the largest indie rock night in London. At first I had problems getting into a good mood. It was too crowded for my taste, and the girls didn't really appeal to me. Plenty of them were trying to get my attention, though. I could not be bothered and just hung around.

A fairly good-looking girl smiled at me. She was really luscious. Too bad that a band came on when I was about to make a move. Somehow I did not quite feel like chasing after her and watched the band instead. After they were done playing I danced on my own for a bit. Then I spotted a group of cute Asian girls and hip-bumped one of them. I am sure she saw it coming because she simulated that she was stumbling down to the floor. She turned around and gave me a huge smile. Somehow I wasn't really interested and did not follow up with anything afterwards.

(When she saw me hooking up with another girl later, she gave me a really angry look.)

Since there was no other club around, my only choices were to either go home or lower my standards. I chose the latter. FRECKLES was certainly one of the more attractive girls in this sea of mediocrity. At first I only noticed a cute face in the crowd. I liked her blonde mane and her full luscious lips. Upon closer inspection I realised that she had a really nice rack. She was a bit on the chubby side, though. It was not terribly bad, but I said to myself that I would not bang her. However, the thought crossed my mind that it would be amazing to watch her suck me off.

FRECKLES was part of a larger group. She looked at me. I took both her hands to pull her in. We made out in no time. Before I could proceed further she interrupted me by asking the usual questions. I gladly answered those while playing with her ass and tits. She was into me but her friends seemed sceptical. I said to her that I felt a strange vibe from her friends but she replied that I should not worry about it. Eventually they sent their only guy as an ambassador. It was easy to befriend him. He told me how awesome he thought Germany was, and that was that. A couple of slaps on the back later we were best friends forever. One of the two other girls came closer. Before she could say anything I spun her around to cheer her up. It didn't help. She remained sceptical. Since I later won over the other girl in the group I had nothing to worry about, though.

I let FRECKLES massage my cock through my pants for a while, nibbled on her neck and squeezed her boobs. Then I dragged her off the dance floor. She was pretty cool. Even better, being an au pair for a rich family in Chelsea, she had great living arrangements. Furthermore, her host family was on vacation. At this point I was sold because I always had wanted to see a rich family's house in London. I kissed her again. Moments later I was rubbing her crotch. This was about fifteen minutes into the interaction, which was rather slow for my standards. On the other hand, she seemed to be a more reluctant girl. When I dropped that I would like to see how she lived I noticed a spark in her eyes. After some more banter I just said, "Let's go!" She wanted to say goodbye to her friends first. One minute later she was back and we walked out of the club.

It took us about an hour on the night bus to get to her place. We exchanged stories as if we had known each other for years. When I dropped that I had a crush on my French teacher, which had caused some embarrassment, she asked me whether she had caught me jerking off in the class room. FRECKLES seemed to be fairly horny already.

Back at her place things went smoothly. I did not want to take her straight to the bedroom because I was hungry. The fridge was full of organic food, and I ate as much as I could. Overall, the house was impressive but there was much less living space than I had expected. Pictures of the family were all over the place. The guy was really chubby, worked I don't know how many hours a week and looked as if he was about to have a heart attack at any minute. I chuckled. Then I helped myself to some more of his food. I really appreciated his work ethic.

After chilling in her kitchen for a while we went upstairs to her room. For a moment I considered dragging FRECKLES into the parents' bedroom, but this probably would not have gone down too well. In her room we got down to it straight away. We laid down on her bed and made out for a while. I fondled her breasts and her right hand quickly found its way into my pants. We undressed each other. She kissed me again and her mouth wandered south. She gave me a truly amazing blowjob. What I had imagined came true.

For a moment I contemplated banging her, but it is so rare to come across a girl that is competent at sucking cock. Thus I happily came in her mouth. FRECKLES seemed addicted to fellatio. I made the most of it and let her give me some more blowjobs that night. We barely even kissed. All I had to do was guiding her hand down and after a few strokes, as soon as there was a bit of blood flow, she went down on me. In return she got a couple of earth-shattering orgasms from my magic fingers. She was multi-orgasmic and it was a real pleasure to watch her getting off. I left her house the next afternoon, after letting her serve me some great breakfast. Later that night I saw CHOCOLATE again and for the first time I found it unbearable that she was not great at sucking cock. I decided to teach her how to do it.

I really enjoyed spending time with FRECKLES and kept her around for blowjobs. This was a role she gladly accepted. She also was the reason I lost some motivation for a while. Sex had just become a tad too available for me. I literally could call her up and she came around. It was like ordering a pizza over the phone, with the difference that I ordered free blowjobs. After a couple of minutes of token conversation she went down on me. It was that simple and convenient. We always hung out for two to three hours and took turns giving each other great orgasms. Every man should have a girl like this in his life. It was the most easy-going relationship I ever had.

Tasting a 19-year-old is sweet for an old fuck like me

It was my first night out in Berlin. My expectations were probably a bit too high, because the club that had been recommended to me would not have survived for more than a couple of weeks in London. It was going strong and their Friday night allegedly had a reputation of being "legendary." Things were really not that great at Bang Bang Club, however. I showed up past 1 a.m. Four girls in front of me were walking in for free. The bouncer asked me whether I was with them, but I declined. I did not want to be associated with boring and borderline ugly 30-year-olds, so I had to pay. Inside things were pretty bad. There was a noticeable surplus of guys and the girls were not that interesting. I already missed London.

A big girl came closer and danced in front of me. Because I did not have anything better to do I spun her around for giggles. Then I walked off. The next girl wasn't that appealing either and had an attitude that would have made the worst London girls proud. Apparently I was in for a huge disappointment. There still wasn't much to do, so I chilled to the music for a bit. Two girls started dancing next to me. I let both grind up against me. The more attractive one tried to get rid of me by saying that her friend really dug me. Too bad I didn't dig her at all. I sat down again. Later this girl apparently changed her mind and sat down next to me, while her friend was dancing quite far away. I couldn't be bothered to talk to her because I don't tolerate bullshit.

Because the fog machine had been put to good use I couldn't see much more than two feet ahead. In order to get a better view I climbed the stage. A girl was smoking a cigarette. In Germany a smoking ban had been half-heartedly implemented recently. Clubs usually have a smoking and a non-smoking area. She was smoking in the non-smoking area, so I told her to stop doing so. Five minutes later she was dancing next to me and tried to initiate a conversation about smoking, which I found a bit retarded. Upon closer inspection I realised that she did look a lot better than I initially thought. She was really cute. I let Cutie finish her cigarette before talking to her. At first I wondered why she wasn't even pissed off. Being the stuck-up schmuck I am, I attributed it to my dashing looks and suave style. More likely she was intrigued because I told her that I found her behaviour offending. Whatever the reason was, it did not really matter. After about one minute of bantering and letting my hands rest on her hips I pulled her in for a make out. Moments later I sat down on the sofa that was behind us and pulled her down to my lap.

We chatted, made out from time to time and got to know each other better. I told her a couple of stories from my life, what I had done in the last few years and the like. She did the same. The only problem was that she was there with two big girls, and one of them was missing. Her friend Zaftig showed up. I am a chill guy, so I befriended her by asking bog-standard questions and — Take note of this! — some innocent touches on her upper arm. It worked like a charm.

Cutie left to get a drink and, alas, Zaftig sat down right next to me. Apparently I still had to prove to her that I was worthy of getting my cock sucked by her girlfriend. I made random comments about the club and she completely ate it up. Now three other girls were dancing right in front of me and competing for my attention. They were almost throwing themselves at me. It was a bit bizarre. One of them stepped on my foot, then turned around and bowed down before me. Even better, about a minute later she sat down right next to me at the armrest of the sofa, literally begging me to do something. I did not feel like risking to ruin the pick-up of Cutie and let this opportunity pass. In one last attempt to get my attention she leaned back and thrust her chest out. This made me feel an urge to talk to her, but I was able to control myself. Seconds later she buggered off because Cutie came back and sat down on my lap.

Cutie lived in a nearby town with her parents. Getting to her place would therefore have been a real pain in the neck. Luckily it would only take me twenty minutes on public transport to get back to my place. This was not at all like in London. I told her that I was wondering what we should do. She asked me to clarify, but I just kissed her. After this little break I said I was thinking about going home. With audible disappointment she asked me whether I really wanted to. I replied I did and invited her to come along, in a completely casual tone of voice. It took her a few seconds to come up with an answer. Eventually she said, "Yeah, we could do that." But first she had to find CORNFED so that ZAFTIG would not get too bored in the club. She told ZAFTIG what the deal was and she did not object. A little bit of friendly conversation apparently goes a long way. CUTIE walked off again and left her handbag with me, just as before when she was getting a drink, so there was no need to worry about her not coming back.

Another girl sat down on the armrest of my sofa. It was getting ridiculous. She was hotter than CUTIE, but it would have been foolish to jeopardise the pick-up at this point. It was a shame because she was dying to get into my pants. She was leaning into me, gave me a huge smile and almost fell into my lap. I just sat there, looking straight ahead, without even acknowledging her presence. When I gave her a glimpse, she leaned back in response and thrust her tits out in an attempt to get my attention. She was pretty, probably a bit tipsy, and out on her own. It does not get better than this. Even though she was in her late 20s, there was nothing to complain about. I sincerely hope someone else picked her up that night. Otherwise it would have been a severe waste of talent. Well, you can't have everything. Besides, CUTIE was 19 years old and looked like the chicks in *Barely Legal*. There really was not much to complain about her either.

CUTIE came back with CORNFED in tow. Just to be on the safe side, I thought I better talk to her for a bit as well, but CUTIE quickly interfered with, "Let's get out of here!" She dragged me off, without giving me a chance to even say goodbye to her friends. Apparently someone desperately wanted to get laid tonight. I'm afraid there isn't much else to report about actual "game." We walked to the nearest station. I kept her in her horny and inquisitive state and then we arrived at my place.

So far I had always ended up at the girl's place, so I felt a bit insecure at first. The bigger problem was that I was sleeping in the room of my flatmate NUMBERS who was on vacation. Mine was still occupied otherwise. To prevent any kind of situation I told her about it and that the room therefore was a bit of a mess. She did not complain when she saw it and probably did not care about it anyway. I offered her some water and came back with two glasses. Upon returning I took a sip. She didn't. Instead she shoved her tongue down my throat. Seconds later we were on the bed, undressing each other.

She left at 2 p.m., after a couple of decent orgasms, a thorough massage and a few hours of sleep. I really enjoyed being with her, despite some issues in the bedroom. CUTIE was literally ravishing me and I got turned on so much that I ended up ejaculating prematurely. Anyway, it was an awesome night and I enjoyed truly connecting with her. Besides, being 29 and pulling a girl ten years younger feels pretty damn amazing. By the way, her pussy was completely shaved, which only confirmed my suspicion that she had hoped to get laid. She was not overly experienced, but this did not matter much because I really liked her.

I did see CUTIE again and we entered a relationship that lasted for about six months. Eventually she ended it because she could not deal with the fact that I was seeing other women on the side. I just increasingly neglected her. When I think back I consider it a shame because you don't often meet girls you really like, and I really liked her. She would have deserved to be treated better.

Against considerable resistance

Unemployment certainly has its benefits. For instance, it allows you to go out on a Tuesday night and not give a damn about anything. On the way to Bang Bang Club I spotted two cute girls in the tram. I had a hunch that they were going to the same club and I was right. They were somewhat appealing, but a bit out of shape. I will refer to them as my groupies in the following.

I entered the club past 1 a.m. To my great surprise there were only about fifty people in there and this number did not change much throughout the night. The music pretty much sucked, so I preferred to chill on one of the sofas. Thirty minutes later a couple of dolled up girls walked in, but I knew them already. It was amusing that I kept bumping into some girls I regularly ran into before leaving for London in 2006. Not all of them had aged well.

I was not in the mood to approach any of the girls and walked around disinterestedly. Suddenly TEASE bumped into me from the side, which caused her to spill a bit of her drink. She playfully slapped my arm and said I should pay her some money to compensate for her loss. This sounded too much like bullshit to me. Because I had not yet realised how marvellous her breasts were, I did not pursue this opportunity further but went to the dance floor instead. My groupies showed up and danced around me. One of them kept staring at me. When I acknowledged her presence she raised her drink. For a short moment I considered going after her but decided against it. Sitting down on the stage seemed more appealing to me.

Cougar sat down an arm's length away from me and looked over. I held eye contact, which prompted her to coyly slide up to me. She leaned in. I could have made out with her instantly, but I didn't. Instead I offered her my neck. She immediately sunk her teeth into my scruff and sucked on it. She did a good job. My groupies witnessed this and were visibly shaken. I'm a completely chill mofo, so I leaned back and enjoyed the attention I got. Cougar took a break from sucking my neck. I yanked her head back and bit hers. When she tried to say something, my suspicion that she was wasted got confirmed. She stood up and slowly walked away. Apparently I could have left with her. Probably she had just said something along those lines but I could not quite understand her. I remained seated because I didn't find her attractive enough. Because I had not followed her, she came back and angrily told me I was "apparently too stupid for this." Little did she know. She must have left the venue afterwards.

After this rather amusing intermezzo I was in an extraordinarily good mood. Tease showed up out of nowhere to dance right next to me. I spun her around and pulled her in to make out with her. My groupies could not believe this either. To my great frustration this girl seemed to be only interested in making out. She blocked all my attempts at having a conversation. Against considerable resistance I dragged her over to a sofa. We got to know each other better, but only on a physical level. When I asked her for her name she replied with, "Now, why would my name be important?" However, since she was the only girl I considered worth pursuing I decided to stick it out.

Minutes later we were back on the dance floor and continued with our little game. I increasingly pushed her limits: scratching, biting, hair pulling, crotch rubbing — you name it. She quickly got into it. In a sincere tone of voice I asked her whether she liked all this. TEASE gave me a huge smile but denied that she did. The rest of the seduction was along very similar lines. I made her horny and gave her a chance to release some tension. Then I pushed her away some more. My actions were flawless. (Yes, I am a conceited twat.)

I asked her where she lived. She did not want to tell me, so I retorted that I would find out later anyway. It took me a quite some time to wear her down. The process was almost mechanical and somewhat rhythmical: we danced, I dragged her to a sofa, then we made out for a bit and eventually I told her that we should leave. I must have taken her through this routine three or four times. Every time, though, she shook her head and said she could not take me home because she didn't even live in this city (bullshit), because she was staying with friends (bullshit) or because she lived far out (bullshit). I thought I was on the right track, considering that she gave me a different reason every time, while keeping her hands running up and down my body under my T-shirt.

TEASE pulled out some tobacco, so I led her outside. She told me that she was thinking about taking next year off to travel the world (bullshit) and that she would like to take me with her (bullshit). She was dangling off me the whole time. I felt that I had won the battle. All that was left to tackle were logistical problems.

It was close to 4 a.m. Tease said she had to find her friend Butterface. It turned out that she was busy with some random guy. Thus she asked me to dance with her some more. I completely dominated her and she loved it. I pulled her in and bit her neck hard. She shoved me away forcefully. I walked up to her slowly, grabbed her hair, yanked her head back abruptly and made out with her while I still had a bunch of her hair in my hand. My groupies were watching in disbelief. She was sweating and her horniness was completely obvious. After this episode we sat down on a couch again. Tease had severe problems restraining herself. Without having to give her any guidance she put her hand down my pants and whacked my cock. I would have been surprised had I not gotten her that night. There wouldn't be many surprises anymore. It was a done deal.

While she was whacking my cock, a bouncer interrupted us and told us that the club was about to close. It was fairly dark so I doubt he had seen what was going on. Outside we hugged and made out some more. Tease dropped that she lived with nine other people (bullshit) and that she would not take me home with her (bullshit). Her friend Butterface showed up with the guy from before. It seemed that he was about to get lucky. After he had rolled cigarettes for the two girls we all made our way to the train station. I took my girl's hand and led her there. She said that she appreciated that I want to walk her home, but that she had to leave me soon (bullshit). A train arrived. It was Tease's, but she was too late to realise it. Or maybe she just didn't want to take the train with me in front of her friend. Thus

I had to endure some more minutes with Butterface and the other guy. The next train arrived minutes later and on we got. Oh, I almost forgot, Tease also said that she was sharing a flat with Butterface (bullshit).

A few stops later we had to change to the underground. There she kept spouting out crap, saying that she could not take me home (bullshit), but that she was glad I had decided to "walk her back" to her flat. Note that we were virtual strangers. Our complete conversation would not even have filled a single page. All I had done so far was keeping her horny so that she had to chase me to get a release.

At the underground station I put her hand on my crotch and let her rub my cock for a bit, before taking it away. I asked her, again in a very sincere tone of voice, whether this made her horny. Tease looked deeply into my eyes and said it did, but "only very minimally." (Of course, sweetie!) On the train she laid down on the seats, with her head resting in my lap. Less than ten minutes later we had arrived at our destination. Once again she said she really appreciated that I was walking her home. I wondered whether she actually believed any of the bullshit she was trying to feed me.

Her flat was close to the station. She wanted me to lead the whole way. We were holding hands and she gave me the directions, so that I could drag her there. In front of her house she stopped and said that now would be my time to ask for her number, and that she would expect me to do so (bullshit). I told her I was thirsty and would really appreciate if she offered me a glass of water. I had thought I would never get to use this line. Tease agreed but said that I would have to leave immediately afterwards (bullshit) because she was tired and had to go to bed (bullshit). At long last we entered her flat. (She was living alone, by the way.) The first thing I did was taking my shoes off. She made a disparaging comment about my winkle-pickers, which I ignored.

I sat down on the couch in her living room while she got me something to drink. Because she had nothing but alcoholic beverages at home she could only offer me tap water. Not that it mattered in any way. Moments later she joined me on the sofa. I took a sip of water before making out with her. She asked me whether I had deliberately used the pretence of wanting a glass of water to get into her flat. Instead of answering her question I gave her a stern look. TEASE finally cracked and laughed. Apparently there is only so much bullshit a girl can tell you before admitting to herself that what is happening is exactly what she wants. Things got hot and heavy in no time. Less than two minutes after entering her flat I was already sucking on her juicy knockers. It did not take us long to end up in her bed — and in the morning I realised I didn't even know her name.

Taming of the shrew

Public indecencies

Despite being in a happy relationship with CUTIE, I felt like going out. At around 1.30 a.m. I showed up at Magnet Club. Once again I completely stood out because in Berlin most guys have no clue how to dress. Almost as soon as I walked in a girl tried to grind her ass against my groin. Her boobs were great but a quick look at her body made me stay away from her.

After accidentally wasting my time on girls with boyfriends and doing my best to avoid a physical confrontation I went to the dance floor. The reason was DOLL, a really sweet girl. After hovering around her for a bit she stopped dancing and smiled at me. After smiling back I took her hand. A couple of minutes later I tried to kiss her. She said I was "a really good dancer, but this doesn't mean that I want to take this any further." I later learnt that DOLL was in a relationship that was in its eighth year already. (She was in her mid-20s.) Her friend MAUVE got suspicious and cut right in. DOLL told her it was fine and that she would like to continue dancing with me.

I saw a great opportunity and immediately switched to MAUVE. She was much more aggressive than DOLL and apparently in greater need of male attention. On the dance floor she was very bold. For instance she deliberately lost her balance, forcing me to catch her. After a couple of minutes we made out. Moments later I dragged her off. She resisted a bit, but I have a firm grip. When we got into the hallway she tried to provoke me with, "Oh, the hallway, how classy!" I just pushed her up against the wall and made out with her.

MAUVE was unwilling to engage in any kind of conversation. Occasionally she even completely ignored what I said. All she wanted to do was make out with me. She said that nothing would happen, that I should just forget about it and that she had to get back to her girlfriend. However, her hands were all over my body. When she wanted to walk off I took her hand and led her back inside. I thought my best bet was to be more dominant. It was time for hair pulling and the like. In response she said this was too much for her. Her every action betrayed those words, though.

I leaned against the wall and pulled her in. Things were progressively getting hotter. I put her hand on my crotch and she rubbed it. Again she said she could not leave her friend alone for so long. She kept talking and told me she was only visiting and had to leave in two days. Then she rummaged her handbag for a business card, but she didn't have any left. I took her number instead. At this point her number would have been worthless, even though she reiterated that I should call her the next day. I finally let her go.

She wanted me to chase after her, but I didn't do her the favour. Instead I sat down on a sofa and chilled for a bit. A cute blonde girl sat down next to me on a really uncomfortable wooden table. I had noticed her staring at me earlier tonight, but I didn't feel like talking to her. Mauve reappeared in my vicinity and kept glancing over. We exchanged smiles. Two songs later she walked up to me to ask whether I was up for "one last dance." The tables were about to turn.

I pulled her down into my lap right away, and her demeanour changed completely. Suddenly she was rather submissive. We talked about a couple of things, discovered biographical similarities and common interests. I did a quick evaluation of the situation. She had told me that she was staying with Doll who lived in a small flat. Therefore the only plausible options were sex inside the club or taking her back to my place. I decided to think about it later. First I had to get her horny enough.

I took her back to the dance floor. One thing led to another and suddenly we were scratching and biting each other. Eventually I led her off to a small and semi-hidden lounge area. There were only two sofas there. Someone was sleeping on the first one, but the other one was unoccupied. I threw her onto it and made out with her while rubbing her crotch. In between the make outs I told her she had marvellous breasts (she did). She gave me a beaming smile in return. I also said I would love to suck on them (which I did do later). All this caressing, kissing and squeezing her boobs and ass had quite an effect on her. Her hands were all over my body, then under my shirt and finally in my pants, fishing for my cock. I pulled it out to make her job easier.

Mauve had taken quite a liking to my cock and visibly enjoyed whacking it. She said she would love if I sucked on her nipples and slightly pulled down her top and bra. Her breasts were amazingly well-shaped. I sucked on her juicy tits, played with her nipples and bit them. This made her moan heavily. I didn't want to push her over the edge, though. After she blurted out that she would love to suck my cock I grabbed her head and tried to push it down there. She stopped me and said she couldn't do it because we were in public. As I said before, the two options were the toilets or getting her back to mine. The toilets at this place were disgustingly dirty, so I didn't really feel like taking her there. But she didn't seem to like my suggestion to go back to my place either.

That I had been on the right track became blatantly obvious when she, out of nowhere, spouted out, "Finding someone to have sex with isn't exactly a challenge." I retorted that this was correct, but that it is nonetheless great to be intimate with someone you really like. She wanted to impose that she was the selector and that I could at best try my luck. (The next day, though, she said she was glad *I* had picked her.) Then she asked me when I last had sex. I nonchalantly told her that it was just two or three days ago. When I asked her about herself, it took her a bit longer than expected to come up with, "Last Sunday." I wasn't too sure whether she was telling the truth. She pressed her body against mine, looked deeply in my eyes and said, with a bit of concern in her voice, "Please don't tell me you are in a relationship!" I did not consider my relationship with CUTIE a typical one so I truthfully declined but told her about CHOCOLATE. Her hands were on my cock all the time, by the way.

MAUVE had a great eye for my arousal and made sure I was getting less than I was craving for. She also made a very impressive finish. I told her to jerk me off to completion. She nodded and after gently touching my cock for a bit she gave me a great handjob, moving her hands faster and faster. When my cock began to throb, however, she abruptly stopped and said, with the voice of a little girl, "I have to go now. Sorry!"

It was about 5 a.m and the club was about to close. One phone call later we met her friend Doll outside. I told Mauve that I would come with her. Doll laughed and said that she had a really small flat but if I didn't mind her listening I could come with them. She was not serious about it, though. Doll addressed Mauve to tell her that it would be perfectly fine if she left with me. This was apparently contradicting the rules they had agreed on. In a faux-embarrassed tone she replied, "That was not at all what you should have said!" Their tram soon arrived. Mauve kissed me goodbye and said I should call her. Her friend also suggested I should call Mauve, which I found amusing.

"Problems all left alone..."

I got up at 2.30 p.m. the next day and called Mauve after breakfast. She was excited to hear from me and exclaimed that she had not expected me to call. Because she hadn't made any plans yet, I suggested to meet me at 5 p.m. at St. Oberholz, a cafe in a central location. We parted more than ten hours later.

I was on time, but she had been early. It was an amusing coincidence that we both had independently ordered a glass of ginger tea. I jokingly commented that this must be fate. At first Mauve tried to keep some distance by putting her handbag in between us. I immediately put it to the other side of the sofa. Minutes later my arm was around her and I pulled her closer to me. The vibe was good from the get-go. Of course I couldn't continue where I had left off the night before. Nonetheless, the situation looked promising, especially when she randomly blurted out that she really loved the way I had sucked on her nipples.

She would not let me massage her head, though, and she didn't want to kiss me in the cafe either. I tried it a couple of times, but I thought that there was no rush as we had plenty of time. After all, it was still broad daylight. Mauve finished her tea quickly and drank the rest of mine afterwards. She was playing with the glass virtually all the time. Somewhere I have read that girls do this when cocks are on their mind. I got hard. She suggested we go for a walk.

There was a little park nearby. It was quite deserted, so I figured that her inhibitions would be much lower. After a spontaneous spin I pulled her in and we made out for a bit. From that point onward I made sure to kiss her from time to time to keep her in a happy mood. Soon she initiated make outs herself. Apparently Mauve was fully aware in which direction the interaction was going because her nonsense just kept coming. When I wanted to sit down on a bench she commented that this was such a cliché and when we passed a playground she suggested that I had only taken her there because I expected her to be impressed by it. This was a theme she harked on for quite a bit. Another example was her asking whether I took all my girls to this particular park.

Nonetheless I was pushing things forward steadily, which made her comment that, "We are moving a bit too fast." For my standards we were actually moving fairly slowly. Because we had hung out in this park for about an hour already I suggested going back to my place to cook something. At first she completely ignored this statement. Twenty minutes later, however, she said that she was "really hungry." At the tram station she seemed to get second thoughts or maybe she only tried to get a reaction out of me by saying, "I'm sorry, but I don't think you're my type." She did not object to my fondling her breasts at the same time, so those words had no impact. She steered back and said, "We could go back to your place, but then we'll only cook and nothing else. Promise?" I could agree to that.

Unfortunately my flatmates had friends around. Cooking in front of four or five other people did not strike me as the best thing to do. We only said "Hi!" to them and went straight into my room. MAUVE inspected the place and randomly commented on a number of things. It was cute. I told her to take her jacket off. She didn't want to take off her boots, though.

Moments later I was leaning against the wall and pulled her close. I did not react to her objection that she was really hungry. We made out. I lifted her up and threw her onto my bed. After some cuddling and talking our clothes subsequently came off. Her boots eventually did as well. We fooled around for a while. She was fairly experienced, and I was impressed by her response when I told her to show me how quickly she could get herself off. Her claim was that she could come faster than any man. I don't know about most men, but she could get herself to an orgasm through clitoral stimulation within one minute. I did not even have any work to do. We cuddled for a bit afterwards. After kissing for a while I gently pushed her head down. My cock ended up in her mouth. She was quite good at it. Unfortunately she had some hang-ups about her period.

During post-coital bliss she told me about her likes and dislikes. Eventually she steered the conversation towards the topic of relationships. She told me that she was still in the process of getting over her boyfriend of six and a half years. They had split up over a year and a half ago and she felt that she was still not able to meet someone new. I thought that she was on the brink of getting too much into me, but she said there was no danger because our "arrangement" was just perfect since we lived 600 kilometres apart.

About two and a half hours of physical and verbal intimacy we got ready to leave the flat. I asked her whether she wanted me to cook something for her now but she preferred going to a restaurant instead. I had to go to the bathroom first to get presentable again. When I came back I saw Mauve texting Doll, "We've just left the flat and are going for drinks now." Apparently she had made further plans already. I'll keep the rest short. We went to a nice restaurant and she acted cuter and cuter as the night progressed. She was quite unlike the person she was when I first met her. I liked it. One of the highlights was her taking a couple of pictures of me while commenting, "This is just for me. I hope it's okay with you." I also appreciated that she paid the bill. Well, she was one year younger than me but had a well-paid job so it was only fair. Afterwards we went to another cafe and spent some more hours cuddling, kissing and talking. What I liked most about her was that she had a *joie de vivre* many people possess in their childhood but gradually lose as the grow older. You don't often meet people like her.

We parted after 3 a.m. I walked home with a warm and fuzzy feeling inside, not knowing whether we would ever see each other again. This did not distract from the joy we both had found in each other. Maybe it was a perfect day.

We kept in touch. After exchanging a couple of playful emails she spontaneously called me and invited me to her place. Some weeks later I took a flight. We spent a great long weekend together.

An orgasmic early morning in a park

I had not gone out for about one month because I was busy with other things. Then my girlfriend Cutie insisted on going to a club with me. I had a blast, even though I felt very constrained. Somehow I severely pissed her off and got her to the brink of leaving without me — and I had not even hit on any girls! If there was one thing I have learnt then it was that I missed pulling girls. I made a vow to go out the very next day. Cutie had stayed at my place until the afternoon and she made me cum three times. I wanted to go out nonetheless.

My flatmate Numbers is pretty cool for a mathematician. He is in an open relationship, but I am probably just a jerk who doesn't mind cheating on his girlfriend. (Then again, we never talked about our status.) I told him about my itch to go out and he joined me. Past 1 a.m. we showed up at White Trash, yet another indie/electro joint that claims to run the most fashionable indie night in town. In this case it could well have been true, but it was still falling short of London standards. The music was not bad, but there was much to dislike. The fog machine was in constant use and the sound system was one of the worst I had ever been exposed to in a club. To compensate for the lack of sound quality, the DJs cranked the volume up to eleven, which made having conversations rather difficult. The worst of all was the lighting. My pink T-shirt looked grey. Only my white belt stood out. It had the atmosphere of a rave which is possibly the worst imaginable setting for picking up girls. I don't mind a challenge, though.

The first girl I bumped into triggered a massive déjà vu. I remembered her because she was one of the first girls I had made out with virtually instantly and she also was one of the most attractive girls I had made out with by that time. Besides, I have the memory of an elephant. (We are talking about around May 2006 here!) I walked by and Déjà Vu bumped into me. She wanted to know who I was but I was sure she had recognised me.

After some bantering I dragged her off to a secluded area I had discovered earlier. I explored her body with my hands and it did not take her long to squeeze my ass. Déjà Vu wanted to give me bits of her life story, but I told her she was a huge cocktease and only wanted to lead guys on. At the same time I was fondling her breasts. She threw in that she was "so not like that." In response I pushed her against the wall and made out with her. I should have been much more aggressive and tried to get her out of the club quickly. Instead we made out for a bit, chatted and joined her friends after about fifteen minutes.

I certainly enjoyed her grinding her ass against my crotch and running her hands over my body. But somehow I thought that it would be a good idea to walk over to Numbers to talk to him for a while. Afterwards I had difficulties finding Déjà Vu. I eventually spotted her at the bar with one of her girlfriends, and joined them. They were about to go upstairs. I said I would come with them. But I didn't, because I had a feeling that this girl meant a huge amount of work. When I bumped into her about an hour later she was not willing to acknowledge my presence anymore. She made out with another guy and then with yet another. However, she eventually left the club alone. As I said, she was just a huge cocktease.

I approached a couple more women. The first one wanted to dance, but she quickly got a bit uncomfortable. This is a common problem when dealing with very young girls who are in the company of equally young girlfriends. After a while the second one told me she "actually" had a boyfriend. I replied that she should not worry because I was in a relationship as well. This seemed to be a rather bad line because she turned around and walked off. The third one looked spectacular from three meters afar, but close-up she was not great at all. A couple of women in their mid-thirties were around as well. They were just waiting to get picked up. One of them still looked really good. Well, her face had a few tiny wrinkles, but she had a tight body. I did not have to fall back to this option, though.

On the dance floor I witnessed a girl rubbing some guy's crotch with visible delight. I thought I better find myself one to do the same with me. BADONKADONK, a girl with a really cute face, huge knockers and a bit of meat, but not too much, walked past. She was apparently looking for some attention and I was willing to give it to her. I grabbed her wrist and pulled her close. She quickly wanted to make out with me. I made her wait and put her hand on my crotch. She eagerly rubbed it. Feeling how my cock got hard was apparently too much for her, so she walked off. I grabbed her hand and pulled her in again. We hugged and moments later I shoved her hand down my pants. Skinny jeans aren't that great for handjobs, so I had to pull my cock out for her. She did not seem to mind stroking it but said something along the lines of, "I don't normally do this," and that she "must apparently be really drunk." (She wasn't at all.)

After my cock had gotten hard from stroking she let go of it and told me she could not do this here because, "You'd have all the fun and I'd have to clean my clothes." I got the hint and moved her over to the nearest wall. Thanks to the fog in the club we were now almost invisible. I put my cock into her hands again. BADONKADONK said she had some hang-ups with hook-ups and that she did not really feel comfortable in such situations. But this was not at all what her gently rubbing the head of my knob suggested. She fired off the usual questions. We talked about a couple of things, age, what we did and all that boring crap. I could take it because she was stroking my cock at the same time.

I told her that we should go somewhere else. She objected. I tried to drag her off nonetheless, but she wouldn't let me. A few minutes later I told her again that we should continue this somewhere else. Even though she initially objected, she followed me willingly. Outside the men's toilet she gave me a speech that she had outgrown "things like this" and that I should "look for any 18-year-old who would probably come with you in an instant." Girls always assume you could get *any* other girl with no problem at all, but it's not that simple.

I described how great it would feel for her to have my hard throbbing cock in her hands. She was listening eagerly, but when I said that she could also suck on it she tried to make a scene. A hug and some caressing took care of that problem. A guy bumped into her and spilt his drink on her forearm. BADONKADONK told me to lick it off. I refused, which made her complain that if I expected her to suck my cock I should at least be willing to lick off her arm. She had a point and I licked the vodka off her skin, even though I don't drink alcohol.

It was time to get her into the men's toilet. She objected and said she did not even knew who I was. I replied by giving her my name and asking for hers. Then I said, "Now that we have settled that...," and lead her off. I almost would have made it into the stall with her. Some random guy entered it shortly after we had come round the corner. We had to wait outside for a while. More guys walked in to take a leak. BADONKADONK could stand the pressure of one guy pissing in front of her, but when there were suddenly three guys standing there she walked out. "This is too much for me," she said and tried to get away from me. I don't give up that easily, though. I grabbed her wrist, pulled her in and we hugged for a while. After some comforting things were getting a bit better. Then a friend of hers showed up. I high-fived her and she was quite friendly towards me. They walked off to dance. For a moment I thought about coming with them but I had to piss first.

Ten to fifteen minutes later I got really bored of this club and wanted to leave. I looked around to find BADONKADONK. In passing I tapped her on her shoulder and waved goodbye. She gestured me to come closer and told me she was really sorry for having made "such a fuss" and that she would have loved to let herself get carried away. I smugly said she could make it up to me some other time. She nodded and looked at me with gleaming eyes. We exchanged numbers. I tried one last time to get her out of there but she objected because of her friends or work the next day or blah blah blah.

As luck would have it I bumped into BADONKADONK again at the underground station about twenty minutes later. She immediately ditched her friends to come talk to me. It turned out that we shared a bit of the way. She had to get off one stop before me and invited me to "walk her to the tram station." On the train she was a bit distant, but that was because her friends were sitting nearby. We got off the train and moments after it had dispatched we were holding hands. Some girl threw me an interested glance while I was walking past with her.

At the tram station I pulled her down to sit on my lap. Almost immediately I began to rub her pussy through her jeans. At the same time we were talking about life and other things. She also revealed a bit too much information for my taste, like the fact that she was a bit of a mess because her mother had recently killed herself. To get her off this topic I said, "Even though you may think you have problems expressing your sexuality and feeling trust, I believe you are a very passionate woman who just needs to give herself permission to enjoy herself." It was cheesy but it did the trick. This was a turning point in the conversation, but she still didn't want to take me back to her flat. When the tram arrived she suggested to "walk around the block instead" and added that she hoped I was fine with it, "even though we won't end up devouring each other."

I took her hand and walked with her in the direction of my flat. Unfortunately I had already told her where I lived. She quickly figured out what I had in mind and protested. We took a turn and walked towards a park. I suggested "hanging out" in there. Needless to say, the moment we sat down on a bench things got hot and heavy. It was past 5 a.m., it was dark and there were strangers walking past occasionally, which only added to the thrill. BADONKADONK was sitting next to me. I lifted her legs up to rest on my lap. After some kissing and caressing I pulled my cock out and she proceeded to give me a truly amazing handjob. I am a bit of an exhibitionist, which made it all the more enjoyable for me. Eventually I blew a load. It was the best orgasm I had in months.

It was my turn to get her off. She did not let me unzip her jeans, though. On the fly I came up with an effective solution: I rubbed my knuckles hard against the area where I thought her clitoris was. Under normal circumstances I find it easily, but if you have a girl in her jeans in front of you there is some guesswork involved. However, by observing her reactions I could figure out how close I was. I put some effort into it and achieved quite a bit of stimulation. She moaned louder and louder. It took me a while, but eventually she came hard.

After some shared post-orgasmic bliss we chilled and talked for about thirty more minutes. She was a cool girl. In reference to the fact that I moved to Berlin only recently she said that I would "experience things like this more often." Pretending that it was some kind of regional custom to publicly whack off strangers apparently helped her to justify her actions. It was around 6.30 a.m. and we were both freezing. Not only was it cold, we were also tired and hungry. I walked BADONKADONK back to the tram station. She suggested to share a cab back to her place, but I could not be arsed because I was getting really tired. I preferred to walk home because I only wanted to go to bed.

I thought about what else I could have done in the park. It struck me that I could just have stood up and put my cock in her mouth. It could have worked had I warmed her up sufficiently. It is easy to hide mutual masturbation in public, but fellatio is a different case. However, her writhing, aching and moaning was also impossible to conceal. Anyway, it was a great experience. I am still not sure whether this constituted cheating on my girlfriend, though.

More indecencies

I was certainly having a lot of fun these days. One thing I did not have enough of, though, was sleep because I was seeing three girls regularly. I couldn't be bothered to return the calls of one of them today, however, because I preferred scoring some food. Earlier that week I chatted up a guy on the underground for giggles. He offered to invite me to dinner. My suspicion was that he wanted to pound my ass, but I don't play on that team. He took me to an expensive Italian restaurant and I certainly appreciated the food and conversation. I still wanted to fuck, though, and went to a club afterwards.

My "girlfriend" Cutie had to work this weekend. It would have been stupid not to exploit this opportunity. First I went to a party at Humboldt University, which sucked. There I bumped into Aristo-Dud, a random acquaintance of mine. He made my ear bleed with stories in which he alluded to the wealth and connections of his family. When I told him that I was about to leave for greener pastures he wanted to come along. I did not really mind and invited him to join me. On the way to Bang Bang Club he told me that he had fucked his girlfriend the night before. I wondered why he bothered telling me this and had problems containing my laughter while listening to his bullshit.

Inside the club I went to the dance floor. Juicy noticed me and moved closer to me. I suspected that she had pinched my ass moments before. She looked very seductive with her long fake blonde hair reaching down to her ass and makeup which would have made any pornstar or hooker proud: bright red lips, black mascara, an awful lot of black eye shadow and a bit of sparkle on her cheeks. Because I was not up for settling that early I scoped out the club first. About ten minutes later she did her little dance in front of me again. I thought, "Fuck it, let's go for an easy lay and pull this one." I spun her around, let her grind her pussy against my thigh and dragged her off to a sofa afterwards. Less than five minutes into the interaction she was stroking my cock while I was rubbing her pussy. I can't remember whether I had also fingered her at this point. I probably did. The actual amount of our conversation was minimal. She asked for my name and I asked her where she lived. Juicy claimed my place was too far away and that we could not get back to hers either because her parents were visiting. By the way, she was an exchange student from the UK.

Ten minutes later I told her to get her stuff so that we could "go for a walk." On the way out I caught a glimpse of Aristo-Dud. He was about to pull Juicy's heavy friend. This was great because he tremendously eased my task. How could her friend cockblock me when she was about to get some dick herself? Aristo-Dud had bad manners, though. He tongued his girl down openly while groping her in the most obscene ways imaginable. I do have some tact and don't squeeze boobs and buttocks in broad public. Most of the time, at least. Now imagine a scrawny guy working on a big girl and you can understand why I wanted to get out of this place quickly. Well, the real reason of course was that I wanted to continue with Juicy.

My girl realised that her friend was safe. She quizzed me on Aristo-Dud for a bit and I told her that I did not really know him but that he was a really good guy. (I hope you did not disappoint me, asshole!). At around 2 a.m. we were outside in the blistering cold. She really did not seem to want to go to the train station, so I dragged her over to a bench instead. Moments later she was rubbing my cock, standing in front of me with her blouse open and shoving her tits in my face. I love these horny girls! I undid her belt and put my fingers up her cooch, making her moan loudly. Between moaning she raised the objection that there could be people passing by. Juicy was a bit of an exhibitionist, just like me, but her objection was valid because the bench was in the middle of a rather open area. Thus we walked off, trying to find a better spot.

I noticed a staircase leading down to the bench of the River Spree. The stairs were wide enough for us both to sit down and they hid us well. We continued were we had left off. Juicy told me she doesn't suck cock on the first "date" when I was trying to put it in her mouth. I am fine with taking things slowly, so I reached for a condom. All the time she was stroking my cock and telling me how much she loved it. I slowly put two and then three fingers into her, while squeezing her boobs with my other hand. She was out of control. I pulled her panties and trousers down to her knees. The next step would have been to slap the condom on and getting down to it. Too bad it was really cold. Within seconds she had pulled up her clothes again. Truth be told, it really was cold with temperatures below zero, and therefore I couldn't blame her for her instinctive reaction.

I told her to sit down right next to me. My cock ended up in her hands again and she whacked me off to completion. Then I gave her an orgasm with my magic fingers while telling her dirty things. After some post-coital bliss we went back inside the club. I really loved the way Juicy looked: her hair was all messy, her makeup smeared all over her face and her clothes were in utter disarray. I had jizz on my coat, so we definitely made a great couple. On the way she told me that she never does such things and that she was "actually a good girl."

Back at the club she first fixed her appearance, which took her about fifteen minutes. Apparently I had done a thorough job. Afterwards she wanted to dance and show me off. I'm fine with giving a bit of validation if I get my way, so I went to the dance floor with her. A couple of songs later we sat down again to cuddle and talk. She was a cool girl to hang out with, but I didn't like her self-important arrogance. She dropped that she knew "everybody" in this club. I don't really react to such nonsense, and fingering girls from behind usually takes them off such threads anyway. It also worked in this case. While I was hitting her G-spot with my middle finger she smiled and moaned. Because I did not want to get her off again I let my finger linger inside her. This probably reminded her of something and she asked me whether I knew Mike Skinner. He is a musician that is better known by his stage name The Streets. She insinuated that she was important because of her connections. She also alluded that she had hooked up with him and wanted to show me some of his text messages. I was already bored of it, so I asked her completely nonchalantly whether she had fucked him. Realising that I was utterly unimpressed she immediately went back to vibing, followed by more caressing and playing with my Johnson.

I was amused when she blurted out that she knew me from another club and jokingly told her that I must have made quite an impression on her. Later on I remembered when I had seen her.

The only thing about her I could remember were her boobs, though. I saw her the night I had a fight with my girlfriend Cutie who complained that I wasn't giving her enough attention at the club. My repeated attempts to get Juicy out of the club didn't go anywhere. She kept telling me that her parents were staying with her and that she had to get up early the next day. At around 4.30 a.m. I told her that we should go. This time she quickly packed her stuff and left with me.

While waiting for the train I kept rubbing her crotch, and she did the same with me. She repeatedly said that she was really horny and suggested to meet up again another day. On the train some guy realised that what I had on my coat must be jizz and cracked a smile. Juicy apparently liked this, gave me a huge smile and tongued me down. She had some "cock sparkle," as Chocolate called it, on her jacket as well, but I did not point it out to her.

It was a bit burdensome to get to her place. The police had barricaded off a couple of streets for whatever reason and we had to take a detour. Juicy told me more about her parents and that they were going Christmas shopping with her the next day. It struck me that maybe she wasn't bullshitting when she commented that she appreciated my making the effort of walking her home. She repeated that we should see each other again soon and told me where she would hang out on Thursday the following week. She also dropped that I could find her at White Trash the next day. Since her parents were staying for the whole weekend there was no point in going there, though. Besides, I had made plans for that day already, and they involved my girl Blue Eyes.

While we were standing in front of her house it was apparent that she was still extremely horny. She begged me to put my fingers in. Had she been bullshitting about her parents she would have faltered at this point. Girls this horny do not pass on the opportunity of getting cock without a valid reason. But of course she could not get railed by some random guy while her parents were sleeping in the other room. We were thus looking for another way to find a release. She mentioned a nearby playground. On our way there a couple crossed our path. As I have written before, the police had barricaded off the area. She asked us where we were going. I told them that we were "going for a walk." Then she asked, "But where? You can't go anywhere right now." The girl was a bit thick. Her guy just laughed and dragged her off.

At the playground we fooled around some more. Her hands were on my cock again, but there was already too much disturbance. When I was on the brink of busting a nut, a random couple — You effing pensioners! — was about to walk past very close to us. Thus I told her to stop. JUICY was a bit disappointed that she did not manage to stroke me fast enough to make me cum. I gave her some more action with my fingers and made her moan heavily. She came again.

Two women quickly served me at the bar

I had decided to see my two or three regular girls only on weekdays because I wanted to go out regularly again. This made the position of two of those girls insecure because my time is obviously limited. Cutie was still my favourite girl. Blue Eyes was more interesting but not very exciting in the bedroom, and the third girl I honestly can't even remember anymore.

The indie rock scene bored me so I went to Berghain, one of the most famous techno clubs in Berlin. This place is internationally renowned. At 3 a.m. I showed up with my flatmate Numbers in tow. It was open until 5 p.m. and there was a constant stream of new girls coming in, not unlike a horn of plenty that refills itself. For hours there were about as many people leaving as there were arriving. It was amazing. I had a number of great interactions, probably because all the girls were tripping on something. Highlights were a conversation with a divorced and insanely hot MILF about cocks and how much she liked to get fucked, a girl that was afraid her ex-boyfriend would beat me up if he caught us but nonetheless made out with me, and two girls that pulled my cock out of my pants and whacked me off out in the open. This is probably the only one worth writing about.

At around 7 a.m. I spotted a group of girls that looked somewhat familiar. I had met them in January at Watergate while I was on vacation in Berlin. They were heavily flirting with me back then and I probably could have fucked two of them in the toilet. Too bad my skills were nothing compared to what they later developed into. One of the girls, LATINA, made eye contact. I pulled her in for a hug. She asked me where I was from. A couple of sentences later I spun her around so that she could grind her firm ass against me. With her right hand she reached around and massaged my crotch. After a bit of assistance from myself she pulled my cock out. Usually I try to hide it under my T-shirt, but she did not care about that at all. My cock was completely visible and she whacked me in the middle of the crowd. In order to somewhat even the score I pulled down her top on one side and played with one of her fairly large breasts. I felt alive.

LATINA commented to her girlfriend CHEEKY that she liked my cock. Because she was smiling, LATINA put one of that other girl's hands on my cock. Both were now happily jerking me off. Their three other girlfriends were excitedly watching. Within moments people took notice and stared at the scene with a mixture of disbelief (males) and horniness (females). I was hugely turned on by it. Yet, it was a bit too much for me. I had done some pretty crazy things, but with the situation at hand I could not quite deal with. However, I was confident that I would get more tangible results in similar situations next time. It was an amazing experience nonetheless. I felt like the man. Then I felt that I was about to cum.

I considered it bizarre to blow a load in front of about a dozen spectators who were watching those two girls whacking me off in unison. I gestured the girls to stop and put myself together again. For a few minuted some of the girls that had been watching hovered around me with beaming smiles on their faces. I had to get a grip on myself again first, so I blew these opportunities. Realistically speaking, though, I think I could have taken any of them to the bathroom straight away.

Latina was a bit annoyed and backed off. I sat down on a stool because I had to come down. Her previously uninvolved girlfriends now took turns rubbing my crotch. They did some playful things like putting each other's hands on it. It was quite amusing. Then another guy sneaked in and chatted up Latina. He took her to the toilet in less than ten minutes. Considering how horny she was he could have achieved the same ten minutes earlier. Twenty minutes later she came back, not wearing her tights anymore. I found it quite stupid to stick around and checked out the new girls that had arrived in the meantime.

Roughly two rather uneventful hours later I decided it was time to go home. It was around 10 a.m. already anyway. I spotted Latina again and walked up to her to say goodbye. We hugged and then she scratched my crotch. What a horny girl! Then she pulled my cock out again. I dragged her off to a secluded space, but things were a bit odd there. She was extremely wild and apparently on a dangerous cocktail of drugs. We sat down. After some cuddling and mutual masturbation she suddenly got up, lifted up her skirt and tried to shove her crotch in my face. I was not having any of this and pulled her down again. She got a bit fed up and stopped caressing my cock. We cuddled some more and I kept playing with her fake breasts. In the process I apparently ruined one of the straps of her top. By now I felt we were done here. The reason was not that I had ruined her top, but that I refused to lick her pussy. Cuddling with such a hot girl, however, is also fine for a couple of minutes.

Cheeky suddenly joined us. Now I had one girl to the left and one to the right. However, Cheeky had found a new guy in the meantime. Right in front of us she pulled his pants down to his knees and tickled his cock with her pointy black leather stilettos. I found this to be fairly hilarious, but it also turned me on. This went on for a while. Then she just walked off, letting the guy stand there like a complete idiot. Latina was getting tired and said she wanted to leave. She had to collect her friends first, though. I was not quite up for trying to pull her home. After all, I suspected her to be one of the worst skanks around. Therefore I did not even bother to get her contact details.

I ran into Latina again about six months later at the same club. It was a very interesting encounter, to say the least. But I'll save this story for another day.

A 16-year-old sucked me off in a toilet. Thrice.

My girl Blue Eyes recently thought she could give me some shit. I had to dump her. In principle I was thus looking for replacement. However, in the last few days I had gotten more sex than I could handle because Cutie was on a horny streak. My motivation to go out and pull new ass was therefore quite low. It was New Year's Eve, though, and I had already bought tickets for an indie/electro night at Magnet Club. My flatmate Numbers was with me as well.

We rolled up past midnight. To our great surprise there was a noticeable surplus of women and many of them were good-looking. It took me some time to get used to the venue but after twenty minutes I was already dancing and spinning girls around. Peach tried to make her way through the dance floor. I stopped her and put her arms around my neck. We made out within less than a minute. I quickly dragged her into the hallway and said we should go to my place. More making out ensued. She objected because it was "quite early still." After rubbing my crotch for a while she left to find her friends, but made clear that I should wait for her and that it would only take her about ten minutes.

I don't like to sit around idly, though. Peach was rather good-looking, but not top of the line. Some others, however, were. Therefore I decided to continue working on her only if I accidentally bumped into her again. Having put this question into the hands of fate, I prowled the other dance floor. It was a bit too packed, so I stood at the periphery, wiggling my hips. Stripes stared at me. She was a complete stunner. We moved closer and rubbed our buttocks against each other's. I made some room for us on the dance floor. Her first move was to wrap her arms around me. I turned her around so that she could grind her ass against my dick.

Seconds later and after some guidance on my part she was rubbing my crotch. She tried to get her fingers into my pants all by herself. This took too long, so I pulled my cock out for her. I let her jerk me off while I had two fingers up her snatch from behind. After some moments of this I took her to the other dance floor, which was darker. I leaned against the wall and she pressed her body against mine. My cock was fully out and she was whacking it. My friend Cosy recently got whacked off to completion on the dance floor. For a moment I considered repeating this feat. But then it struck me that Stripes was so horny and the circumstances so good, i.e. there were no attendants in the toilets, that I had to see how far I could go.

The obvious next step was to drag her into the toilet. Some weeks ago I had found them too dirty, but I was too horny to care. Stripes had no qualms. Actually, I think she was more than glad that I took this step. You may notice that I did not mention any conversational threads. That's because there were none. The only thing I said to her was, "You seem to really like my cock, don't you?" Like most women she was starving to be around a strong, masculine guy and jumping at the opportunity when it presented itself.

Moments later we were inside the men's toilet. One stall was unoccupied and I ushered her inside. I gestured her to sit down, while I was pulling my pants down. She kissed my chest for a while, moved teasingly downwards and the next thing I know was that she was chewing on my dick.

Fellatio is such a lost art and I had not gotten decent head in months. In London I had a sweet girl just for blowjobs and her performances were mind-blowing. I so missed FRECKLES! Everything I got after that was often mediocre. But not this girl. She sucked on my cock like a pro and with visible pleasure. Unfortunately I did not have a condom with me. I usually keep them in the pocket of my coat. However, considering how amazing she was at sucking my cock I doubt I would have wanted to fuck her properly anyway. My girlfriend CUTIE was quite good in bed, but not so when it came to blowjobs and I certainly appreciated this change. I had problems retaining myself and came earlier than I would have liked. It was still great. STRIPES even kept sucking after I had blown my load and I had to stop her because the tip of my cock got too sensitive. Not many girls are this eager.

It was my turn to do something for her. I turned her around and fingered her to orgasm. It was hot. It was really exhausting. It was hard work fingerbanging her for about fifteen minutes. I repeatedly had to change hands. Afterwards we cuddled in the stall. Post-coital bliss apparently is a strong force. She was completely off when she guessed my age and said I look like 20. Well, thanks, but I was actually 29. When she told me she was only 16 I almost got hard again. Admittedly she did look very young. I took her outside again.

Before I got really good at picking up girls I enjoyed dancing and making out with them for hours. I wanted to relive those fond memories. Because I had just cum in her mouth I was in no mood to either take her home or to look for another girl. Hence I enjoyed my time with STRIPES dancing, caressing, and kissing. About an hour later she received a text message from one of her friends. They wanted to leave. I tried to get her into the toilets again, but she was not having any of it. We kissed and parted.

It took me a few split-seconds to realise that my cock was still dangling out of my pants, so I fixed myself while checking out the rest of the dance floor. The looks of the women in my vicinity were priceless. Some had the "please fuck me right now" look on their face. It was amazing. I could not make use of any of it, though, because someone tickled my back seconds later. It was STRIPES again. She told me her friends would leave in fifteen minutes and that she could therefore stay with me a little bit longer.

I amped her up some more and tried to get her into the toilet again. This time she gave me some shit, saying it was "trashy" and that she could not just go to the men's toilet with me. I bet this was due to her liking me more than when we had first met. Excessive cuddling apparently has this effect on girls. Since she said she could not come to the men's toilet with me, I took her to the women's toilet instead. She barely resisted and when I dragged her in she willingly followed. There was a huge queue inside, so we walked back out again. Then I tried to get her into the men's restroom. After more token resistance we were inside. Lucky us, one of the stalls was empty. I sat her down and, as if she was starving for cock, she wasted absolutely no time. She unbuckled my belt and eagerly pulled my willie out of my underpants. So much for her concerns. I let her suck me off for a while. Then I turned her around and drilled her with my fingers.

Trying to get a girl off this way can be demanding. Not only did we barely have any space, some guys were knocking on the door and there was noise everywhere — and of course the stall was not exactly clean. It must have taken me twenty or thirty minutes. I pulled out some quite aggressive stuff like forcefully grabbing her hair and yanking her head back while biting her neck hard. Damn, this was all so hot! STRIPES urged me, while she was moaning heavily, "Please stop! … Uuuh…. Please! … Aaaahhh…. I…. Aaaaahh…. I can't…. Aaaaaaahh…." Of course, it was impossible for me to stop. Moments later she erupted into powerful orgasms. She seemed to want more. I kept fingering her and made her cum a second time. We were both dripping in sweat. I even had problems keeping my balance. There was a reason I woke up with sore muscles in my arms the next day.

I pulled my cock out of my pants again. Now she was whacking it while I still had three fingers in her. This went on for a while. I turned her around, sat her down on the toilet and put it in her mouth again. She was trying really hard to please me. It was such a pleasure to watch and an incredible stroke for my ego. She must have worked it for easily twenty minutes.

A guy that had to pee urgently kept knocking on the door. A few minutes later he jumped up to see what was going on inside the stall. He shouted, "Hey! There is a dude in there getting sucked off." He was German, but STRIPES was not. She was a tourist from Italy. I was thus lucky that she did not understand the dumb jibes Peeping Tom and his idiotic friends were making. I could not cum under such circumstances and gestured her to stop.

We pulled ourselves together and were cuddling and caressing each other afterwards in the dirty stall. It was a beautiful moment. After a few minutes we went outside and had to endure a couple of stupid comments. Had Stripes understood any of them, she would have felt rather uncomfortable. Peeping Tom was still around, shouting after me, "What took you so long, loser?", as I exited the stall with her in tow. Well, I am not the one who has to resort to porn. I did not even look at him as I did not see the need to acknowledge him.

When I checked the time I realised that we had spent around ninety minutes in the stall. It was past 4.30 a.m. already. So much for her "fifteen minutes." I found us a nice place to sit down. She became incredibly sweet, like most girls do after an orgasm and we caressed each other for two more hours or so. It was such a joy to have this gorgeous sixteen year old girl sitting on my lap, purring and being completely enthralled by me. Stripes was a really great girl and this was one of the most amazing sexual experiences I have ever had. I could not think of a better way to kick off 2009.

I feel it is necessary to point out that the age of consent in Germany is 16. In your country things may be different, though.

www.ingramcontent.com/pod-product-compliance
Ingram Content Group UK Ltd.
Pitfield, Milton Keynes, MK11 3LW, UK
UKHW041826200726
13854UKWH00002BA/610